23tales

APPALACHIAN GHOST STORIES, LEGENDS & OTHER MYSTERIES

EDITED BY
TERRY SHAW & BRAD LIFFORD

HOWLING HILLS PUBLISHING

Howling Hills is an independent publisher of quality nonfiction books.
We're committed to telling stories from Greater Appalachia
and focus on people, the outdoors, food, and the environment.

Learn more and connect with us at *howlinghillspublishing.com*.

EDITING
Terry Shaw and Brad Lifford

BOOK DESIGN
Travis Akard

COVER PHOTOGRAPHS
©Frank Cone, ©Alexander Krivitskiy, ©Eren Özdemir, ©Spencer Selover

23 Tales: Appalachian Ghost Stories, Legends & Other Mysteries
©2023 Howling Hills Publishing

First published in the United States of America in 2023
by Howling Hills Publishing, Kingsport, Tennessee.

Howling Hills Publishing, LLC
Kingsport, Tennessee

ISBN: 979-8-9881621-1-7
CIP data is available through the Library of Congress.

23tales

APPALACHIAN GHOST STORIES, LEGENDS & OTHER MYSTERIES

THESE APPALACHIAN STORIES ARE AS VARIED AS THE REGION

When we put out a call for Appalachian ghost stories, we figured our anthology would be met with both skepticism and enthusiasm. And we knew those reactions weren't mutually exclusive, which is why my publishing partner and I did a blog post on our own views. I wrote that I believed in ghosts. **Brad Lifford** had his doubts.

Now, don't tell him I said this—or at least don't tell his scientist wife—but I suspect the stories we received changed Brad's views.

With our earlier debate in mind, the collection begins with ghost-skeptic-turned-ghost hunter **Matt Sorge**. Over the years, Matt has conducted hundreds of paranormal investigations. "I don't know any of these things with certainty," he writes. "However, I do believe unequivocally in the paranormal and on the most fundamental level, that people who die may leave behind a part of themselves—some sort of energy, a spirit, a ghost—because an experience, grief, or trauma keeps them tethered to this world."

Many of our stories back that up, including the personal experiences of **Donnamarie Emmert** in "Barter Theatre Performance a Fright," **Jennie Ivey** in "A Faint Scent of Shalimar," and **Suzy Trotta** in "Think You Can Sell a Haunted House?"

We also received submissions that could be described as "unexplained," such as **Natalie Kimbell's** quirky "Not Our Exit." The same with **Patricia Hope's** sweet story of her beekeeper grandfather, "On the Wings of Bees."

So rather than sticking to ghosts, we named the book *23 Tales: Appalachian Ghost Stories, Legends and Other Mysteries.* That may not roll off the tongue, but we hope it gives a sense of the variety within these pages.

Many stories are funny, such as **Jeannette Brown's** "Mr. Oldfield's Gift." Others are chilling, including **Candance Reaves'** "The Attic" and **Kimberly L. Becker's** encounter in "The Raven Mocker."

Some have impressive staying power. Skeptical Brad reported on a haunting that's lasted for more than 60 years, through the relocation of Roseland, the historic building now located at Exchange Place Living History Farm in Kingsport, Tennessee.

In fact, history is a common theme. **Kevin Saylor** recounts a lynching in "Haunted Drummond Bridge." **Daniel Stetson Ray** writes about a gunfight in "A Dastardly Liar." **Michael Sobiech** relies on regional newspapers from the fifties for "A Haunting in Bent Creek Cemetery." And **Laura Still** provides a sweeping historical view in "The Lost Valley of Hardin." With "The Suscon Screamer," **Thom Tracy** mixes local history, legend, and a fair amount of skepticism.

We also share many family stories, such as **Chrissie Anderson Peters'** "West Virginia Turnpike Hitchhiker,"

Patty Parker Ireland's "The Light at Sweetwater Creek," Sue Weaver Dunlap's "Her Voice from the Ridge," and Sherry Poff's "Singer in the Woods." And **Karen Gentilman Clopp** tells of her mother's premonitions in "Things Only She Could See."

Karen's story is set in Kane, Pennsylvania, which brings up another issue. Whether you pronounce it Ap-pa-LATCH-a or App-uh-LAY-sha, people like to argue about its boundaries. The Appalachian Regional Commission defines Appalachia as 423 counties across 13 states. For this collection, we have stories from six states, stretching from the Keystone State to Georgia.

Did we stretch the traditional boundaries of Appalachia? In a few spots.

Though he now lives in Johnson City, Tennessee, **Daniel Peacock's** childhood story took place in Southern Georgia—not the state's hilly north. And people will argue that Williamson County, in Middle Tennessee, isn't Appalachian. But anyone who has ever heard the author of "With Ghosts, Swearing Helps," will know **Judith Duvall** is a daughter of this region, whether she's cursing at you or not.

Trust me.

In the end, we think you'll like this mix of stories.

———

TERRY SHAW, *cofounder*
Howling Hills Publishing

— Contents —

— CONTENTS —

No.

— ONE —

A SHADOW IN THE ATTIC OF DEERY INN

Blountville, Tennessee

———

MATTHEW SORGE

I spend a lot of my free time obsessing about dead people.

That obsession has taken me on countless roads, driving hundreds of miles from my home in Kingsport, Tennessee. It's what led me to the gloomy attic of old Deery Inn in the dark hours of a fall night in 2021.

Other people were with me in that two hundred-year-old attic in Blountville. And something else was with us, too. Not a living person. Something.

We stood in the dimly lit attic, not long before midnight. Twenty feet away from where we gathered, a dense, deep shadow outline of a human being stood near a stairway. The figure moved across the hallway, and a few seconds later, crossed back into view.

For several seconds the shadow moved from one side of the room to the other, approaching two stairwells on opposing sides of the room but not descending. We didn't move, didn't speak. The figure did not come closer to us. Though there was no face and no eyes, only blackness, I felt as if I were being watched.

Fingers that had been grasping my arm pinched tighter and tighter, like a death grip. You could hear a pin drop.

Many adults can point to an experience that sends your life veering off in a radically new direction. Long before my encounter with a shadow figure in the attic, I had such an experience. Though it was seventeen years ago, it feels like yesterday. It happened late one fall afternoon near an old farmhouse on the outskirts of Johnson City in the northeast corner of Tennessee.

I had no belief whatsoever in ghosts and not much interest. Back then, tell me about your ghostly experience and I would listen politely—but belief was out of the question. I might ask a few questions because ghosts and history almost always go hand-in-hand and exploring history had long been an interest. My passion for history is what led me down a couple of country roads, through a tunnel, and out to that Johnson City farmstead, dating to the nineteenth century and cradled in a little valley.

With a day off from my job as a firefighter, I was relishing some time alone to explore an old site that might yield out-of-circulation coins, antique jewelry, or other artifacts from the eighteen hundreds. I parked in a field and set to browsing the grounds with a metal detector.

I came upon an old farmhouse. The two-story relic clearly could have housed a good-sized family decades ago but was now abandoned and crumbling. I could peer a little into the first floor and saw the infrastructure was in bad shape. I turned my attention back to the grounds in front of the house, sweeping with my metal detector. Then a feeling made me turn back to the house and look up.

In a second-floor window, an elderly woman in a blue dress, her hair wavy and gray, was looking down at me. I just stood there—I didn't know what to do. And then, as God is my witness, she literally vanished. She vaporized.

I stood still another few seconds in shock before I started thinking rationally again. And I did what any red-blooded adult man would do in that situation: I ran away from the house, threw my shit in the truck, and took off.

In the Deery Inn attic, the shadow figure kept us entranced. That included me and a colleague, Wes Spurgeon, and at least a dozen other people who were visiting Deery Inn with a specific purpose in mind: We *were* actively looking for ghosts.

From one side to the other, the shadow continued to move across the room. Finally, it stopped at the left stairwell and loped off down the stairs. The silence broke:

We heard the sound of feet striking each step in descent, then the pounding of feet racing across the floor below us. I held my breath as I heard footsteps coming up the opposite stairwell. We stood where we were, shocked and unmoving—but the shadow didn't emerge back into the attic.

The woman next to me was grasping my arm to the point of cutting off the circulation. She whispered: "Did you see that?" Both Wes and I said, "Yeah, we saw that." Everyone in that part of the attic did. We could not explain it, but it happened.

Nowadays, seeking experiences like this is part of my everyday life. I'm a founding member of the Southern Research Society (we call ourselves SRS for short), and there is good reason to conduct paranormal investigations at Deery Inn, once a primary waystation for nineteenth-century travelers moving west on the Great Stage Road through Tennessee.

After William Deery acquired the log home property in 1801, he transformed the expansive building into a trading post, inn, and tavern. It was an important place of the times, and thousands of people stayed there through the years, including presidents Andrew Jackson, Andrew Johnson, and James Polk, and the king of France, Louis Phillipe Orleans.

The SRS has investigated Deery Inn on several occasions and found it to be one of the most active places in Northeast Tennessee. We have captured voices with an electronic voice recorder that detects noises on frequencies lower than the human ear can hear. On the second floor, multiple members of our team—as well as guests we have guided through Deery Inn—have felt an unsettling presence inside a second-floor room. We believe it is the spirit of a woman who once stayed in this room designated for female travelers. Visitors who sense this presence are more likely to be women—my wife has sensed a feminine, despairing spirit near this room. She will no longer go *inside* the room.

What I believe: William Deery has not left the inn because of things unfinished in his earthly life. The woman on the second floor is the spirit of someone who was assaulted there or worse. I don't know about the shadow figure, though a stain on our collective history is a possibility. Prior to the Civil War, prosperous travelers on the Old Stage Road would have sometimes traveled with slaves, and historical research suggests slaves might have been forced to sleep in the attic. I fear some anguished soul may have been that shadow figure in the attic.

I don't know any of these things with certainty. However, I do believe unequivocally in the paranormal and on the most fundamental level, that people who die may leave behind a part of themselves—some sort of energy, a spirit, a ghost—because an experience, grief, or trauma keeps them tethered to this world.

Eighteen years ago, I could've never predicted I would feel this way. The SRS includes nearly a dozen people from all walks and professions of life. We have conducted hundreds of paranormal investigations at historic sites, public places, and private residences in several U.S. states. We look for data that can confirm that a phenomenon is unexplainable, and honestly, most of it can be explained by normal causes. As much as 95 percent can be explained.

That other 5 percent keeps us searching. We conduct occasional investigations where we invite the public to join us—like the one at Deery Inn. We do these to offer a little education and collect fees we turn over to these wonderful historic museums. We're history buffs at heart and want to help preserve these places that connect us to the past.

Ghost hunting is the most expensive hobby I'll ever take on. And, as you might expect, members of the SRS and other folks who explore the paranormal deal with a little ridicule and eye-rolling—I even catch some of it in the fire hall. It's OK. Most people are light-hearted and polite about it, so I take it in stride.

In the end, the expense, the time, the sideways glances— it's all worth it.

I'll keep searching and trying to understand the unexplainable. Though I do expect that I'll never have another experience that resonates like that first one, where the elderly woman stared at me and vanished before my eyes.

A few weeks after that happened, I worked up the courage to visit the man who owned the property. I had found an old piece of jewelry I thought he might want— it belonged to one of his ancestors, and he accepted it with gratitude. I asked him if anyone had reported any mysterious experiences while visiting the farmstead. He said, sure enough, others had reported strange things, though he didn't have any specifics. He told me I was welcome to go back to the house and look around.

So I did. Standing in the doorway of the farmhouse, I confirmed what I first thought. The stairs to the second floor had long ago collapsed—there was no way anyone could make it to the second floor. The roof above the second floor was mostly caved in, too.

I walked outside. The sun was setting on my back as I looked across the fields, and a shadow passed in front of me. I turned, expecting the farmer had driven over to come and tell me something. I could see more than five acres in every direction.

No one was there.

I have never learned who the old woman may have been. But my life changed that day and has not been the same since.

———

MATTHEW SORGE *has been a career firefighter for over two decades. After the unexplained encounter recounted in this story, he began his quest for answers to the unknown and unexplained. Over the years, hundreds of investigations at some of America's most infamous hauntings and countless residential cases have taught him that paranormal phenomena not only exist but have an impact on those who encounter it. Learn more about him and his work at* **www.srsparanormal.com.**

WEST VIRGINIA TURNPIKE HITCHHIKER

Southern West Virginia

CHRISSIE ANDERSON PETERS

When I was a little girl in the mid-seventies my Papaw Little worked for Ford Motor Company in Detroit and drove home to Tazewell, Virginia, on weekends. He never tired of making the drive—any drive—and often told me driving was his freedom. He wasn't afraid to travel, not even "the turnpike," as Mamaw fretfully called it, worrying about the big rigs and other traffic, especially on weekends. Back then the West Virginia Turnpike was a treacherous, 88-mile stretch of two-lane highway.

Since Papaw didn't get off until late Friday afternoon, it was always long past my bedtime when he arrived back home to us. That never stopped me from sneaking out of bed when I heard him come in. I'd tiptoe down the trailer hallway and slide behind the sofa to get as close to the kitchen as I could to hear the interesting things he told Mamaw about his week away at work, my Mom usually asleep in a chair in front of the television.

One night he came in and I snuck behind the couch like always, but he wasn't himself. Normally chatty and in good spirits, he was quiet. Troubled.

"Arthur," Mamaw started as she set a plate of warmed-up leftovers in front of him, "what's the matter with you? You're so pale. Are you sick? Are you coming down with something?" And she started fussing around his face and head, trying to feel for a fever, the way she sometimes did with me when I was feeling puny.

"No, Dot. I'm not sick. Just—something weird happened tonight on the way home and I can't shake it off."

Mamaw sat down, looking very concerned, and I scooted closer still to the kitchen table, making myself as tiny as I could to slide behind the pole lamp that stood behind Mamaw's coffee table. I loved when Papaw told stories and something told me this one would be super special.

He took a bite of his pork and beans with hot dogs cut up in it, just the way he liked them. He started to talk, then shook his head. "It really spooked me," he almost whispered.

"What did?" Mamaw put her hand on top of his and looked into his eyes.

He ate a couple of bites, then took a long drink of milk from the glass beside him. "I don't know why I'm telling you this. You'll just get upset."

"Why will I get upset? What is it? What happened?"

"I was more than halfway home," he started. "It was real foggy, and I saw this fella hitchhiking."

"Arthur Little! You did not stop and pick up a hitchhiker on the turnpike, of all places!" He had been right about her getting upset. This would set her off all weekend.

"I did," he said. "It was a miserable night, and I just thought somebody ought to be nice to the fella."

"And that somebody just had to be you? He could have killed you or anything!"

"Well, he didn't." Papaw tried to calm her down. "He was actually a real nice guy. He was carrying a Bible, and we talked a little bit about God. I asked him what he was doing out on such a night, and he told me he was out there to give me a message."

"He was what?"

"That's what he told me, Dot. That he was out there to give me a message. And I said, 'Look, mister, you don't know me from Adam—' And he said, 'Maybe not, but I can tell you that, in a few months, you're gonna be in a bad car accident, and you're gonna wish you were dead, you're gonna be hurt so bad.' "

Mamaw's face went pale and Papaw's hands were shaking as he recounted the tale. "I told him that wasn't funny and he needed to stop talking crazy. He told me God would look out for me, though. All I had to do was believe. Well, I didn't like any of that kind of nonsense whatsoever, and I was about to let him have it." He stopped and looked around the little kitchen of the trailer, like he wanted to make sure no one else was listening. "But Dot, he was gone."

Mamaw looked into his eyes and saw the same fear I could see from my hiding place. "What do you mean— he was gone?"

"I mean to tell you, just that!" Papaw roared. "He was gone! He wasn't in the seat no more! Just disappeared!"

"Surely you had stopped and he got out—"

"No, Dot, I hadn't even slowed down! I was still driving. You know me, I go the speed limit or better the whole way, so I can get home. He was... he was just gone." It took a few minutes for him to calm down again. I was nervous just listening to him tell about it. "I got to the toll booth, and I rolled down my window to pay and the fella at the toll booth asked me if I was okay and I said, 'No, sir, I am not.' And I told him I had picked up a fella that was hitchhiking, with a Bible. And before I could finish telling him, he looked at me and said, 'Let me guess. In the middle of your conversation, he just up and disappeared?' And I said, 'Yeah, how'd you know that?' And he said, 'Mister, I've been hearing this story for weeks now. I can't tell you how many people have picked up a man with a Bible on a foggy night and he disappears in the middle of their conversation. Nobody stops. Nobody slows down. They just look up and he's gone. It's the weirdest thing ever. If I were you, I'd avoid picking up more hitchhikers,' and he kinda laughed. Well, I didn't laugh, I'll tell you that for sure."

Still upset, he ate the rest of his dinner, and I watched him anxiously for a while before slipping back down the hall to my bedroom.

About six months later, Papaw was in a bad car accident, right there in Tazewell, running grocery errands for Mamaw. A fellow wasn't watching and hit his car from behind with so much force that canned goods in a bag in the back seat hurtled to the front of the car and dashed against the windshield, twisting and denting the cans. Papaw's head hit that windshield with great force, too. He wasn't wearing a seat belt, as it was not yet a national law to do so. He tried shielding himself with his left arm as he was thrown forward against the dashboard and windshield but couldn't use that arm to try to get out of the car when it caught fire. He messed up nerves in his hand and arm that never fully healed, even years later after months and months of physical therapy and rehabilitation. Because of those injuries, he had to take early retirement from Ford Motor Company. Although he still enjoyed driving, he quit picking up hitchhikers.

A native of Southwestern Virginia, **CHRISSIE ANDERSON PETERS** *now lives in Bristol, Tennessee. Peters holds degrees from Emory & Henry College and the University of Tennessee. She has placed in contests with Tennessee Mountain Writers, Mountain Heritage Literary Festival, and Chautauqua Festival (Wytheville, Virginia). Her writing has appeared in* Still: The Journal, Pine Mountain Sand & Gravel, Clinch Mountain Review, Mildred Haun Review, Women of Appalachia Project, *and others. Her books include* Dog Days and Dragonflies, Running From Crazy, *and* Blue Ridge Christmas. *She is finishing a collection of memoirs,* Chasing After Rainbows. *She loves travel and anything from the eighties.*

— THREE —

HAUNTED DRUMMOND BRIDGE
Briceville, Tennessee

———

KEVIN SAYLOR

About four miles south of Rocky Top, along Tennessee State Route 116, lies a small unincorporated community called Briceville. The road from the north is a winding stretch of highway, twisting through hills thick with forest. The route is mostly isolated, flanked by an abandoned railroad line and punctuated by the occasional house or trailer. It's the sort of place that feels lonely and unsettling in the daytime, and where you wouldn't want to run out of gas after dark.

Briceville itself is tiny, bisected by the state highway. There are a couple of residential streets. An elementary school, a post office, a library, a Methodist church and a

Baptist church, and that's about it. You won't even find a stoplight.

Once home to a thriving mining community, Briceville is now like a lot of other former coal towns in Appalachia. Between 1900 and 1910, more than 4,000 residents called Briceville home, making it the largest town in Anderson County. But as of the 2020 census, only 334 residents among 108 households live there. The employment rate is 52%.

Just before the outskirts of town, a dilapidated railroad bridge crosses over the waters of Coal Creek. The trestle is less than 100 yards from the highway but hidden by dense overgrowth and difficult to find unless you know where to look.

Locals say after dark the ghost of a murdered miner walks the railroad tracks atop the bridge.

According to legend, the spirit is that of Richard Drummond.

Drummond, a former sailor, was part of a labor uprising in the early 1890s called the Coal Creek War. The conflict began when mine owners replaced their workforce of paid miners with convicts leased to the mines by Tennessee's prison system. Finding themselves unemployed, the incensed miners destroyed prison stockades, burned mine properties, and freed hundreds of prisoners. Tennessee Governor John P. Buchanan called the state militia to restore order to the valley and hundreds of miners were arrested for taking part in the rebellion.

On the night of August 7, 1893, after the violence seemed to have died down, a soldier named Private William Laugherty and one of his fellow enlisted men received furloughs and visited a brothel in Briceville. The story goes that miners surrounded the house and shot out the windows. Laugherty was struck in the head by a bullet during the melee and died. The other soldier escaped under a volley of shots and reported back to his commanding officer, who dispatched 25 enlisted men to the scene. The miners fled.

In retaliation, early on the morning of August 10, a mob of soldiers overtook a boarding house in Briceville and dragged young Richard Drummond to a nearby railroad trestle. They hanged Drummond from the bridge by an inch-thick rope until he died.

Witnesses differ about whether Richard Drummond was even involved in the shooting of Private Laugherty. Some said he was the ringleader of the mob that killed the soldier. Other witnesses, including the owner of the boarding house where Drummond lived, said he was at home in bed at the time Laugherty was killed. In any case, Drummond was punished for the crime.

As it was, Drummond had a reputation around town for being a less-than-savory character. Some months earlier a Knoxville court had fined him $100 for selling liquor without a license. He also had a reputation for fighting and was known to dislike soldiers.

Sixteen officers and soldiers were later arrested for Drummond's murder.

Today, the bridge has a reputation for being haunted. You can still walk across it, some of the beams now soft from decades of weathering, and see the notches from the rope in the wood. Locals say at night you can sometimes hear the sounds of a struggle coming from the railroad tracks, as well as the desperate final gasps of the miner. Others say they've seen a ghost pacing the bridge at midnight and heard the swish of rope cutting through the air. Some have taken photos at the bridge and later found another figure has mysteriously joined the still scene. Others report odd animal behavior and say dogs won't go near the bridge, as if an invisible fence marks off the area.

During the day the bridge looks like a place where bored, small-town teenagers dare each other to spend the night. But whether any of them are brave (or foolish) enough to camp with a ghost is another question entirely.

———

KEVIN SAYLOR *is the product of a misspent youth watching* Unsolved Mysteries *and* Friday the 13th *movies and reading J.B. Stamper's* Tales for the Midnight Hour *books. So far he's never seen a ghost. But he is father to three messy children, which is basically the same as having a poltergeist.*

No.

— FOUR —

THE LIGHT AT SWEETWATER CREEK

Philadelphia, Tennessee

PATTY PARKER IRELAND

Late at night, just off Foshee Road in Philadelphia, Tennessee, a strange light floats softly over the waters of Sweetwater Creek. Over the years, it has been seen by neighbors, fishermen, campers, teenagers looking for adventure, paranormal investigators, and members of my own family. Those who experience it claim the light drifts and bends across the lonely waters, eventually hovering near a sweetgum tree whose exposed roots dig deep into the soil at the creek's edge, until, at last, its ethereal glow disappears into the darkness. They say the light initially seems gentle and pure. Yet if a person looks directly into it for a prolonged period, so the legend goes, one will see the form of a young, naked, bloody man, his face contorted with pain, his piercing eyes pleading for help. Inside that light he writhes and winces, dragging behind him a long, thick rope tied about his waist. The figure trapped within is purportedly that of my father's Uncle Silas, who died mysteriously in the early 1940s.

I recount this story now as it sounded when my father first told it to me during the spring of 1973 as we visited the old Parker farm off Stockton Valley Road. I was only a teenager at the time, but the tale remains an integral part of my memory and heritage.

Silas wasn't right. You couldn't leave him alone.

If you didn't tie him up to that tree yonder, he'd wander off and get in trouble. It's the only way you could work the fields and get anything done around here in the daylight.

In those days, all the land to the east of the house was crop fields. And the house itself, well, it wasn't brick back then. It was just plain wood siding. We had a big barn over yonder—I guess they tore it down—and a chicken house out back and a spring house over that-a-way. But that big old tree, it's still standing and looks much as it did at the time.

You could watch Silas pretty good from there. If he started to hollering, you could usually holler something back and get him calmed down.

He'd say, "I'm the king!"

Then you had to say, "Good morning, your royal majesty!"

Or he'd say, "I'm bigger than the king. I'm *boss* of the king!"

And you had to say, "Morning, Mr. Bossman."

Sometimes you could distract him by giving him a hoop from a barrel that he could twirl around with a stick or half an apple or one of Edith's old dolls. Once he chewed a glass eye off one of them—swallowed it right down. But it didn't hurt him.

You couldn't let him whittle. No sir. We tried that. If you gave that boy a knife, even if it was just a plain pocketknife, he'd wind up sticking it in his shins or slicing his arms up. You might not even know he'd done it for several hours because he could sit there real calm and serious as a preacher or get up and jump around and grin like a vaudeville clown and, either way, never let you know he was bleeding.

Sometimes he'd holler out his foolishness for half the day and then finally settle down underneath the tree and pull his knees up close against his chest and rock.

You had to give him enough rope so he could climb that tree. He liked to go up as far as he could and sit on a limb and look way off over that line of pines to the west there. That was where the Galyon house was. Sometimes, because he had so much rope, he'd walk around the tree in circles until he got himself tied up; then you'd have to stop whatever you were doing and go over and get him untangled.

People thought it was cruel, but if you didn't tie him to that tree, he'd get away, and then, no telling what. He got loose one day and wound up in a bear trap. Edith and Marguerite nursed his foot for weeks and Granddaddy was afraid the gangrene might set in, but Silas came through. After that, he dragged his left leg along for the rest of his life.

The main thing he'd do when he got loose was go off to the Galyon's and pound on their door and scare their youngest girl nearly half to death with all his loud, crazy talk about how he'd been exiled from a far-off land. And sometimes he'd take off all his clothes and dance around naked as a jaybird hollering out her name: "Catherine! Catherine Anne Galyon! Oh, Miss Pretty Face! Miss Princess Mouth! Miss Hair-the-Color-of-Saltwater-Taffy Catherine Anne Galyon! Come out and kiss me!" He'd pound on her bedroom window, and she'd hide under her bed, shaking, crying, and praying. And then, of course, old man Galyon would call the switchboard operator and say "Hettie? Get me through to the sheriff. Pronto." One time when the sheriff couldn't come, the old man came charging out the front door and started shooting. Silas had sense enough to run home then.

He was harmless, but other people didn't know that. He had a good heart, just no wits to go along with it, to make sense out of his heart to the rest of the world.

"Rufus?" he'd say to me after suppertime, "Can you sing it? Can you sing the 'lights' song?"

> *When the lights go on again all over the world,*
> *And the boys are home again all over the world,*
> *And rain or snow is all that may fall from the skies above,*
> *A kiss won't mean 'goodbye' but 'hello to love.'*

When Silas got loose, we'd stop plowing. We'd go out, as always, searching, pleading, calling his name like a benediction in the twilight, into the low clouds that draped around the heads of the blue ridges like a mourning veil.

"Silas?"

"Si-LAS?"

"Siiiiiiii-las!"

The day it happened, it was hot and sticky—mosquitoes everywhere. You could hardly get your breath.

I was the one doing the plowing. My head was low. My breath was coming hard. The sweat was beading up on my eyebrows and dropping down in my eyes, and I swear when I looked at that tree, I thought sure I saw him huddled up underneath.

But it was just a pile of his clothes.

I noticed after a while that he didn't rock back and forth or holler. I thought he was tired because he stayed up till all hours the night before pestering Granddaddy, wanting to listen to Bob Hope and the Pepsodent Show on the "magic box," as he called our wireless.

"They ain't on right now," Granddaddy explained.

"Well, make 'em come back then," Silas insisted. "Shake that magic box so's they'll come back on again."

"That ain't how it works, son, and that box ain't magic."

"Yes sir. Yes, it is!" He pointed at the large radio sitting atop an oak table that first belonged to my great grandmother. "That right there is true, pure magic, and don't you say it ain't or I'll get sad and mad all at onct."

By the time we realized Silas was no longer tied up under the tree, it was past noon.

Granddaddy said, "Get to the Galyon's. That son-of-a-bitch-bastard's liable to shoot at Silas again like he done the last time."

The Galyons swore they hadn't seen any sign of him.

We combed the nearby hills and the neighbor's fields.

The sun started going down. We went back to the house and got lanterns and walked half the night looking, calling.

No sign of the exiled king.

Don't you know it was three days later before a fisherman found him bobbing, mossy and putrid, his rope tangled up in some logs near the edge of Sweetwater Creek nearly three miles away?

He was twenty-eight years old with the mind of a six-year-old child, and somebody shot him in the back. Old man Galyon denied he did it to his dying breath and no one could ever prove otherwise.

The neighbors over on Foshee Road near where the body was found swear up and down that Silas haunts Sweetwater

Creek, especially the old folks.

They say, "See that sweetgum tree bending over the water yonder? You can see a strange light moving along slow-like right there—right in that spot sometimes late of an evening."

Then they say, "If you look at that light straight on without turning away, sure enough, you can see him a stumbling around inside it."

They go on: "And in the midnight hour, if the wind is just right, you can hear him a callin' out for help."

Toward the end of their stories, they usually add a word of wise edification: "Dying moments is kindly strange like that. They echo along back to us, like a cry from the hills."

Younger folks smile in their mocking way and reason, "There's a logical explanation for where that light comes from."

Old folks smile back and always have the last word: "Don't matter where it comes from. 'Cause where that light's a going, sooner or later, we'll all go."

As for myself, I've never seen that light, but I do like to think some part of Silas remains. In the sound of leaves maybe, or the hush of twilight, or the stirrings of the creek water. Mostly, I like to think that somewhere a light is turned on for Silas now. That somehow, the exiled king is finally home, and someone beautiful greeted him with a kiss.

———

Benjamin, Bennie, Sol Marcus and Eddie Seller. "When the Lights Go On Again (All Over the World)." Benjamin Bennie Music Inc., 1942.

———

PATTY IRELAND *holds a master's degree in creative writing from the University of Tennessee Knoxville and is associate professor of English at Pellissippi State Community College, where she directs its Young Creative Writer's Workshop. In addition to writing fiction and poetry, Ireland is a lyricist/composer. Her work has appeared in* Still: The Journal, 100 Days in Appalachia's "Creators and Innovators," *and* Appalachia Bare, *among others. She is currently writing a novel and a debut memoir entitled* East Ridge As Eden, *which chronicles her story of growing up with a mother who suffered from early-onset Alzheimer's disease and an uneducated but wise Appalachian father.*

BARTER THEATRE
PERFORMANCE A FRIGHT

Abingdon, Virginia

———

DONNAMARIE EMMERT

For over a quarter of a century, I have led the Abingdon Spirit Tour. Primarily, I tell some of the town's history, sprinkled with anecdotes and whisperings of the ghostly activities of our main street. I am the Haint Mistress, and over the years, many of my patrons have claimed to see "something" in windows, taken pictures of orbs, and otherwise have convinced themselves they have experienced paranormal activities. I deny no one's claim, because many years ago, I had my very own encounter.

Long before the renovation of Barter Theatre, I was a theatre major at Virginia Highlands Community College. And I got a call from Barter, asking if I knew how to run sound. I lied copiously and said I did.

Barter hired me and very quickly learned I had indeed, um, *overinflated* my skills. In short, I was awful. The show was *Dames At Sea*, and the sound effects were quite important. I never got them right.

One evening before a performance, I went to my stage manager and asked if, after the show, I could come in and practice. Her name was Champ Leary, and she believed this was the very best idea she'd ever heard from me. "Please, please, practice. But I will tell you this, you will be the only one left in this building. No one else will be here. You will be alone."

Failing to understand what she was actually trying to tell me, I nodded in agreement. She proceeded to give me my instructions:

"Stay as long as you can. When you are finished, stand up and turn out the lights." (The sound and light booth were together in a room at the back of the balcony.)

"When you come out of the booth, pull the door shut," she added. "It's a self-locker, so it's a no-brainer. Come down the stairs. When you get to the lobby, you can't go through the front doors because they're chained shut. You have to get out through the theatre itself. When you get up on the stage, put out the night light." (Every theatre uses one, and it's most appropriately named the ghost light.)

"Go downstairs through the dressing rooms, out the door onto Actor's Alley, and you're done," she said.

That night, after ruining yet another production, I waited until everyone had left and began to practice. Well, I use that word loosely. I was twenty years old and not much for diligence. What I actually did was run through my sound tapes several times as loudly as they would go. I actually made the antique chandeliers shake. It was glorious!

When I finally finished, I followed Champ's directions. I stood up and flicked out the lights. Down in the theatre, I saw a pale blue illumination. It was just emergency lighting, nothing scary. But, when I left the booth and heard the door click shut behind me, the little hairs started creeping up my neck. You know the feeling you get when something is looking at you? I looked and saw no one, of course.

Whistling nervously, I tried not to rush down the stairs but when I hit the bottom step, I ran to the doors. Ugh! Chained shut! If I could have gotten back into the sound booth, I would have spent the night there, but I was locked out. My only recourse was to go out into the theatre itself.

Standing at the very back of the now foreboding theatre, I felt the little hairs creep all the way to the top of my head. In my bravest voice, I whispered, "Is anyone there?"

No answer.

As I crept down the aisle, I nervously scanned the seats. All were empty. It was then I happened to look up in the balcony, and there he was. Clutched up in the corner like a great large spider, he looked at me and I looked at him. That's when he flew down on me.

I use the pronoun "he" quite loosely because from the waist up, he looked like a man, but from the waist down, he had that long wispy tail like Casper, only this was no friendly ghost.

I screamed in terror and fled. The next thing I knew, I had bolted over a box seat and plastered myself behind the proscenium. My mind was racing, trying to make sense of what I had just seen. I mean... a ghost? They didn't really exist, right?

Then I had my answer. I worked in a theatre, and theatre people are very clever. I stank at my job and had made this production very bad. My fellow crew members had decided to play a trick on me. I knew if I had enough light, I would be able to see a piece of fishing line with a sheet tied to it, a very makeshift ghost to scare the daylights out of me. But where would I find my light?

In front of me was the ghost light. A tall post with a caged lightbulb on top and a very long extension cord at the bottom. I flicked it on and leapt out onto the stage. I pulled that light out as far as it would go. Did I see anything in the balcony now? No. A sheet dropped across the seats anywhere? No. Was there anything in the orchestra pit? No.

I lowered the lamp and looked out again.

There he was, third row aisle seat. He was much more solid, though chalk white, and his arms were crossed as if to say, "Hahaha, *gotcha!*"

I squealed in fright and ran. My feet took wings as I pummeled down the steps into the basement and dashed through the catacombs (our loving nickname for the frightening dressing rooms). I made good time until I hit the back door, and I do mean I hit it. I thought it was an outie, but it was an innie, and like Wile E. Coyote, I hit it so hard I bounced off.

Once outside, the wind knocked out of me and scared, I thought about what I had seen and began to run. I lived many blocks away and ran nearly the entire route home.

When I came to work the next day, I told no one about what I had seen. I felt as if I was close to being fired and didn't need to add being crazy to the list of reasons why. So years passed, I moved away and when I moved back, I made friends with some of the new actors and crew at Barter. Times had changed, and now *everyone* who worked there knew about the ghosts of Barter. Robert Porterfield, the theatre's founder, had been spotted many times, and all the techs spoke of their own special ghost, the one they called The Jerk.

I don't know who my ghost was; I didn't ask for ID. However, I know what I saw, and will stand by this story until the day I die.

So, should you see me at a production at Barter, for some extra entertainment value, keep your eye on me. I'm all happy and excited to see what's going on up on stage, but when it's over, get out of my way. I would step on my own grandmother to not be the last person left inside that theatre.

A veteran of the classroom as well as local storytelling,
DONNAMARIE EMMERT *is best known as the Haint*
Mistress of Abingdon. She earned her undergraduate degree at Emory
& Henry in creative writing, theatre, and English, then her M.Ed at
East Tennessee State University in storytelling. She has led the popular
Abingdon Spirit Tours for over twenty-five years and was named
a Passionate Virginian in 2009 by Virginia Tourism. Whether in a
classroom or in the back alleys, Emmert packs a whole lot of storytelling
and a fair bit of history into her lectures as well as her tours.

No.

— SIX —

WINGS OF BEES

Harriman, Tennessee

———

PATRICIA HOPE

The amazing bond between Grandpa Henry and his honeybees went beyond owner and insect. He protected them. If one got into the house as they sometimes did, he would scoop it into his hand and take it to the door, talking to it like an errant child, telling the bee it must stay outside.

Standing six-foot-six, Henry would gently hold a bee, let it meander around his palm while he explained how they meant no harm and how they wouldn't sting us unless threatened. At the back door he'd release a bee after cautioning it to stay out of the house, and off it would go to the white boxes like row houses against our back fence.

"Tell the queen hey for me," he'd say, chuckling as the bee flew off.

Honeybees are a mystery to many people, but maybe I understand them a little better since I grew up with them. I watched from a safe distance as Grandpa would "rob" the hives, scraping the honey from the comb into clear glass jars to go with Grandma's steaming hot biscuits. Sometimes, he'd give me a piece of comb to eat.

He could spend hours watching the hives or climbing a tree to get a swarm of bees someone had asked him to remove. He had no fear of the bees and could scrape them into his hat and place the hat on his bald head and shimmy back down the tree, climb into his car with the bees flying in and out of the open car window and all around his head. The bees crawled all over his face and head but if they stung him, he showed no sign. He would drive home slowly and put the bees into a hive.

If his bees swarmed while he was gone, Grandma and I knew what we had to do. We'd stand in the yard with wooden or metal spoons beating on pots and pans, which Grandpa said would calm them down and make them "settle." The trick was to help them settle onto a tree limb or bush and not on you.

His love for them baffled us all, and until that day we laid him low no one understood the ability Henry had to communicate with the bees. We were standing in the parking lot of the church at his funeral, watching the hearse

45

come toward us, turn off the road and into the parking lot. A swarm of bees flew just above the hearse. When the hearse turned, the bees stayed with it, around the church to where it parked on the far side. After the hearse stopped, and the doors were opened to remove the coffin, the bees paused, made a little dip over the coffin, then flew off. Everyone was stunned. What had just happened? While we cannot know for sure, many of us believe the bees came to pay their last respects and maybe escort his spirit into the next life.

———

PATRICIA HOPE's *writing has appeared in* Anthology of Appalachian Writers, Chicken Soup for the Soul, Southern Writers, Pine Mountain Sand & Gravel, Agape Review, Pigeon Parade Quarterly, Mature Living, The Gargoylicon, Upper Room, Home Life, The Tennessee Conservationist, The Writer, The Mildred Haun Review, The Skinny Poetry Journal, Voices On the Wind, The Avocet, Weekly Avocet, Tiny Seed, Liquid Imagination, American Diversity Report, Plum Tree Tavern, Blue Ridge Country, Ford Times, *and many newspapers and anthologies. She has edited two poetry anthologies and published two novels, including* Lonely Way Back Home *(2017). She lives in Oak Ridge, Tennessee.*

A FAINT SCENT OF SHALIMAR

Webster Springs, West Virginia

JENNIE IVEY

Just because a house is seventy years old and tucked away in a little bitty town in the mountains of West Virginia doesn't mean it's haunted, right?

And just because that house was the lifelong home of a dearly departed old maid school teacher named Welthea Hoover, affectionately known to family and friends as "Aunt Wealthy" (though she certainly wasn't rich), doesn't mean it's haunted, right?

And just because several middle-aged women spent a long weekend in that house and perhaps imbibed a tad too

much cheap wine and perhaps crossed paths with Aunt
Wealthy a time or two, doesn't mean it's haunted, right?

I once swore there's no such thing as ghosts, though I'd
heard scary stories all my life. Stories that made my pulse
race and my breathing go shallow and the hair on the
back of my neck stand straight up. But until I traveled to
Webster Springs, West Virginia, back in the winter of 1998
and encountered Aunt Wealthy's spirit for myself, I never
believed such stories were true.

My friend Paula, our hostess on the trip, is the great-niece
of Welthea Hoover. Though separated in age by fifty years,
Paula and Aunt Wealthy were soulmates. Both were school
teachers. Both loved to travel. Both excelled at tennis.
They enjoyed the same books. They laughed at the same
jokes. And they loved spending time outdoors in wild and
wonderful West Virginia. When Aunt Wealthy died in 1996
at the age of eighty-seven, a heartbroken Paula inherited
her house. It wasn't long before she discovered that, though
Aunt Wealthy was buried in the family cemetery in the
nearby town of Cowan, she wasn't really gone at all.

Those of us who traveled to Webster Springs with Paula
heard many tales on our long drive from Tennessee. We
heard about the backbreaking work of emptying the house
of Aunt Wealthy's belongings—clothes, broken furniture,
expired food, and piles and piles of books and papers—after
she passed away. We heard of the challenges of plastering
and painting the walls and refinishing baseboards and
hardwood floors. We heard about how complicated and

expensive it was to repair plumbing and electric in the old house.

But those weren't the good stories. Nope. The good stories were about visits from Aunt Wealthy's ghost.

Near the end of her long life, when Aunt Wealthy grew unable to take care of herself, relatives arranged for her to move to a nursing home. When Paula's mother, Ramona, told Paula it looked as though they'd have to sell the house to pay for Welthea's care, a pain instantly shot through Paula's back in the exact same place Aunt Wealthy's back had always hurt. "No, Mom," Paula said. "We can't sell, not now and not after she's gone. This pain is a sure sign she wants us to keep the house and fix it up."

Aunt Wealthy died three weeks later, with a few dollars still left in her bank account, while Paula and Ramona were on an overseas trip. "Hours before we got the call from the undertaker, I knew that Aunt Wealthy had slipped into next realm," Paula said. "I also knew she would never really leave me."

Ramona and Paula and her two young nieces soon began the gargantuan task of disposing of their beloved aunt's things. Needing a break one afternoon, they settled in around the dining room table to play a hand of Old Maid. But no sooner had the cards been dealt when a cool breeze blew across their faces, even though every window and door in the house was closed. Immediately after the breeze died down, they heard a knock at the back door.

"Who in the world could that be?" Ramona asked in a shaky voice.

The four of them crept gingerly to the door and opened it. No one was there. They returned to their card game, though it was hard now to care about who was holding the Old Maid. Minutes later, a loud bump came from upstairs and the sound of footsteps could be heard in the hall. Rushing to the bottom of the stairs, they looked up to behold a translucent, milky-white figure dancing lightly across the hall floor. Paula hurried to the kitchen, grabbed a broom, and dashed up the steps. But though she looked under every bed and searched every closet and even checked behind the shower curtain in the bathroom, she found no one.

"That settles it," she told Ramona and the little girls. "We're NOT selling this house. Aunt Wealthy is here with us right now. And she's telling us to keep it!"

Once the rambling old house was cleaned out, Paula got busy fixing it up to use as a recreation destination. It was the perfect place for kinfolk and friends to gather for snow skiing and hiking and rafting. But Paula never invited anyone, including those of us traveling with her from Tennessee, without first warning that the house was haunted. "Neighbors see lights blinking on and off in the middle of the night," she told us. "They hear the radio playing gospel music at full volume. And sometimes they smell spaghetti sauce, Aunt Wealthy's specialty, cooking in the kitchen."

"Doesn't that scare them to death?" I asked, gulping hard.

"Nah," Paula said. "Mountain folks are tough. They just

say 'Welthea's restless tonight' and then they turn over and go back to sleep."

When we arrived in Webster Springs late on a Thursday afternoon, Paula pulled the car into the driveway, slid from behind the steering wheel and hurried up the porch steps. "I'll turn on some lights and bump up the thermostat while y'all unload," she called over her shoulder.

None of us moved.

"Raise your hand if you think this house is really haunted," I said, looking each of my friends in the eye. No one raised a hand. But no one seemed eager to get out of the car, either.

Paula came back out to the porch. "Why are you still sitting there? Come on in where it's warm and pick which bedroom you want. There are enough for us each to have our own," she said. "Not even counting the room where Aunt Wealthy's little sister died."

When we gasped, she added, "Don't worry. She wasn't murdered or anything. She was disabled and died young. We use her room for storage now."

Still, nobody got out of the car.

"I saw a cute little motel just down the road," Debra said, trying to sound upbeat. "How about if we check to see if they have some vacancies?"

Paula shook her head and held the front door open. "Quit being such babies," she said. "Even if Aunt Wealthy does decide to visit, she won't hurt us. She's a friendly ghost, I promise."

So into the house we went.

Julie was the first one brave enough to venture upstairs. "I choose this room overlooking the front yard," she hollered down. "It's full of books about birds and butterflies. I love birds and butterflies."

"It's yours," Paula told her.

"And something else interesting," Julie said. "I can smell just the faintest scent of Shalimar in here. It's my favorite perfume."

Paula got a strange look on her face. "That was Aunt Wealthy's room," she said. "Shalimar was her signature scent. She told me she wore it because it was glamorous and naughty." Paula grinned. "Can you imagine an old woman who looked just like Aunt Bee saying something like that? But how can the smell still be around? I've scrubbed every inch of this house and painted every wall."

Like terrified kindergartners, we shuffled upstairs and into the room Julie had chosen. Though the scent of Shalimar was definitely there, nobody shrieked. Nobody cried. Nobody went running out of the house.

But I'm pretty sure all of us wanted to.

We unloaded the car, ordered pizza and then walked to the Rite Aid—the only place in town with a liquor license— and bought several bottles of wine. We stayed up late eating and drinking and talking, but we didn't see, hear, or smell anything more from Aunt Wealthy that night. The mood was lighthearted the next morning as we gathered around the dining table to drink coffee and laugh about what scaredy cats we'd been.

"You sprayed Shalimar in your room before we got upstairs, didn't you?" I asked Julie. "As a joke?"

She shook her head. "How could I have known Aunt Wealthy wore Shalimar? Besides, I didn't bring any perfume with me," she said. "But the smell is stronger than ever this morning. It's all over my robe, which I found on the floor. I could have sworn I hung it on the bedpost before I went to sleep."

Sheila and Colleen's eyes grew wide. "Our robes were on the floor this morning, too," they said. When the rest of us announced the same was true for our robes, the huge pillar candle in the middle of the table toppled over and rolled onto the floor. Everyone except Paula screamed bloody murder.

"Relax," Paula said, forcing a smile. "It's just Aunt Wealthy pulling pranks. I knew she'd want to meet my friends!"

Other unexplainable things happened that weekend. Sheila, who was trying to quit smoking and who'd pledged not to have a single cigarette during our vacation, smelled smoke while sitting on the front porch. "Did Aunt Wealthy smoke Lucky Strikes?" she asked Paula.

Paula shook her head. "She didn't smoke at all. But my great-grandpa sure did. Three packs of Lucky Strikes a day. I guess he's decided to pay us a visit, too."

That evening during Happy Hour, when I went looking for a bottle of wine I'd left on the kitchen counter, it wasn't there. We found it the next morning, hidden behind a throw pillow on the living room sofa.

Paula assured us that Aunt Wealthy wasn't opposed to sipping some fruit of the vine on special occasions. "Maybe she's just trying to keep the wine for herself," she said.

And there was our visit to the one-room Windy Gap Schoolhouse, moved from its original location to Holly River State Park to be preserved as a piece of living history. The room is lined with bookshelves. As we perused the collection, Colleen said, "None of this ghost stuff makes sense to me. If Aunt Wealthy's house really is haunted, I need a sign." She pulled a dusty book from the shelf and opened the front cover. DONATED BY WELTHEA HOOVER the bookplate said. Colleen slammed the book shut. "That doesn't mean a thing," she insisted. She motioned toward the bookshelves. "Aunt Wealthy probably donated most of these books." We began pulling books, dozens of them, from the shelves and looking inside. Not one book, except the one Colleen had first chosen, had Aunt Wealthy's name inside. It was the sign that she, and all of the rest of us, needed.

Welthea was definitely with us.

Our West Virginia vacation all too quickly came to an end, and on Monday we packed up and headed back to Tennessee, relieved but a little disappointed that Aunt Wealthy never showed up to say good-bye.

She didn't, however, vacate the premises when we left. In fact, her ghostly presence lingered there for a long time. Just before daybreak one morning, more than five years after our visit, Paula was staying alone in the house. She was awakened by a loud bang. Was someone trying to break in? Strangely, she wasn't afraid. "I couldn't see anything in the pitch black darkness, but I felt a comforting presence nearby," Paula told me. "Then someone wrapped their arms around me in a warm, tight hug. And my nose detected just the faintest scent of Shalimar."

It was Aunt Wealthy, of course, come to tell Paula good-bye.

"I love you," Paula whispered aloud, without a trace of sadness. She was certain that, though the haunting had come to an end, the spirit of her beloved aunt would be with her always.

———

JENNIE IVEY *lives and writes in Cookeville, Tennessee, in a house that (so far) isn't haunted by anything but squirrels and wolf spiders. She has written more than a thousand personal columns for* the Herald-Citizen *newspaper and is the author of two books about Tennessee history and one about Elvis. Jennie is a regular contributor to* Guideposts *publications and to* Chicken Soup for the Soul *collections. And she continues to visit Aunt Wealthy's home in West Virginia, unafraid, as often as possible. Look for her upcoming book of nature writing from Howling Hills Publishing.*

No.

— EIGHT —

A DASTARDLY LIAR

LaFollette, Tennessee

DANIEL STETSON RAY

Many people say the old post office in LaFollette, Tennessee, is haunted. Nearly everyone who ever worked there has a strange story to tell. It's been visited by paranormal investigators and is the first stop on a local ghost tour that operates each October.

So how did a post office become a hotbed of supernatural activity?

On July 24, 1903—thirty years before the post office was built—it all started with an argument involving money, alcohol, and guns. Details are scarce, but witnesses reported seeing two men arguing in the street before one made a bold accusation.

"You're a dastardly liar!"

John L. Smith, proprietor of a nearby saloon, then struck Jerry Jarnigan, a collector for the East Tennessee Brewing Company and former sheriff of Grainger County. Jarnigan's response to being walloped and called a liar was to pull his pistol and shoot Smith in the left shoulder. Stunned, Smith limped away toward his saloon while muttering threats of impending retaliation. Jarnigan went across the street to the Cumberland Hotel, stepped behind the front desk, and waited for Smith.

He didn't have to wait long.

A few minutes later, around noon, Smith stormed inside—with his son Taylor in tow—and the three men opened fire in the popular hotel's crowded lobby. John Smith was shot five more times: once near the heart and four times in the stomach. He collapsed and succumbed to his injuries a few hours later. Jarnigan was shot four times in the torso and died almost instantly. All told, at least twelve rounds were fired, but only one bystander was grazed on the wrist by a bullet.

Taylor Smith was not shot. Jarnigan fired all five of his rounds at John Smith, and all five struck their target. He never turned his gun on John's son.

A local lawman named Peterson arrived just as the shooting ended and saw Taylor Smith flee the shootout. Accounts of what happened next are conflicting. Some say

Deputy Peterson drew his gun and shot Taylor in the back of the head in the middle of the street. Others say Taylor made it inside his father's saloon and hid behind the bar, only for Peterson to enter and call for Taylor's surrender. In the latter account, Taylor laid down his gun, raised both hands, and came out from behind the bar. Peterson then shot the young man in the head, killing him instantly. It is unknown whether Peterson ever faced any consequences for his actions.

In the years that followed, the Cumberland Hotel burned down, the old saloon was demolished, and a post office was built in the saloon's place. Not long after the post office opened, workers became convinced the building was haunted. Windows and doors would open and close by themselves. Lights would flash on and off on their own. Disembodied voices and strange groaning noises were often heard echoing from the basement, along with what sounded like hurried footsteps—as though someone were running. The workers would often go downstairs to investigate, convinced someone had broken in, but they never found anyone. Many times the late night delivery man would see lights on downstairs and swear he saw someone looking out the windows when he arrived at 3 a.m.

Odd occurrences were so common that veteran postal workers often warned new hires about the troubled spirits that lurked inside the building. These ghosts were considered otherworldly co-workers, just another part of the job.

The haunted post office became so well known that a few years ago, a group of ghost hunters visited Lafollette to film an episode of their TV series. Their measuring equipment indicated a large amount of activity near the basement door. One of the ghost hunters (apparently the most skeptical of the group) claimed that upon entering the post office, a voice told them to, "Get the hell out!" So that's exactly what he did. Hearing the last four words Jerry Jarnigan ever spoke to John Smith as he entered the Cumberland Hotel was enough to turn the skeptic into a firm believer of the supernatural.

In the nineties, the government moved its postal activities to a new building, and currently, the old post office—now Postmark LaFollette—serves as a center of the arts for the local community by putting on plays and hosting concerts and art fairs and such. Many of the musicians and actors have their own unusual stories to tell, which always seem to peak just before showtime. Items have been flung off tables, costumes gone missing, and sound equipment gone haywire at the last possible moment for no apparent reason.

So if you ever visit downtown LaFollette, drop by the old post office and have a look around. But if you see a young man hiding in the basement, pay him no mind. It's most likely just Taylor Smith, who after all these years, is still hiding from Deputy Peterson.

———

DANIEL STETSON RAY *lives in East Tennessee and spends his time writing novels, short stories and screenplays. His stories have received numerous awards and prizes, including the Sue Ellen Hudson Award for Excellence in Writing, the James Still Prize for Fiction, and the Jesse Stuart Prize for Young Adult Fiction. Though he's never seen a ghost, he enjoys the stories people tell about them.*

HER VOICE FROM THE RIDGE

Polk County, Tennessee

SUE WEAVER DUNLAP

My women kin have consistently experienced "the sight" and visits from those who have passed on, especially those with deep love and commitment. I grew up listening to these healers and midwives, farmers and factory workers, never once doubting their experiences, especially since I had my first experience with "the sight" when I was three. This is my mother's story from 1937, passed down through the years.

I heard a black cat up on the ridge tonight when I went out on the porch for a few sticks of wood to stoke the fire, dark coming later these days when spring whispers down the holler. A black cat, "panter" Mommy calls it, warning us every night since my baby Dinah and me moved back in with Mommy and Poppy after Etha died. I leaned against the porch post and breathed the clean night air of home, the dirt and soot of Knoxville still lingering in the back of my throat. This restless black cat's cries seesawed between the moaning sobs of a young woman and the distressed crying of a baby. Down the holler the wind sounded the longing wail of a grieving man. Dark claimed the rest of this day. Lonely waited on me inside.

It took a minute for my eyes to adjust to the front room, shadows seeking shelter as the kerosene lamps dimly lit the room. Poppy had closed his Bible and put it on the table near his chair. "That cat still up on the ridge?" he asked as I put a few more sticks of wood on the fire.

"No," I said. "Seems to have given up."

I settled in the cane back chair beside him, both of us enjoying the warmth and quiet of the night. Supper dishes were dried and put away, wood carried in for their early rising, Mommy in the back room tending to the youngest still at home. "Every night since I come home," I said, "that cat's been coming around. A she-cat pining for something. Mommy said that cat is bringing us a message, that it started up a few days before word came about Etha being sick. Sure enough, I believe that cat carries a world of hurt."

Poppy rocked on, like he was trying to take in what I was saying. I breathed his Prince Albert cherry tobacco mixed with soft smoke from the fireplace. After a while,

Poppy picked up his strop and razor from beside his chair, leaned in toward the light lingering around them, and began sharpening his straight razor, his touch delicate and rhythmic, like a bow on his fiddle strings, fingertips gentle on the fret. Tension faded from my worry-filled mind, back and forth. Back and forth. I rocked to the beat of Poppy's movements, blade to strop, back and forth, rest a bit, check its sharpness by running the blade across his left arm, hair sliding away with the razor's renewed edge.

Quiet usually felt natural for us. Tonight, he sensed my mood, both of us still gripped in grief over Etha's death. Poppy couldn't quite grasp his daughter was dead. I had lost my sister—my best friend. These cold evenings cut us to the center with a hurt neither could catch hold of, let alone deal with, the nights always the longest when Etha seemed to be walking through our dreams.

"You decided what you're going to do about Walt?" Poppy said, breaking the silence. "He seems set on you marrying him and raising Etha's babies. It ain't right, you know, those babies being in that home for orphaned children. They got a daddy."

"I couldn't stay with him, Poppy. People talking about us like we was nothing but trash. And Walt just sitting around day in and day out, grieving himself over Etha and their baby Kenneth dying. Dinah and me needed to be out of there. No job. No food. No ambition. I want no part of it."

I didn't tell Poppy about me loving Walt and him belonging to Etha. How I had carried that love for years. And I'm not going to live second-best to a dead woman.

"Well, girl," Poppy said. "I reckon you forgot that promise you made to your sister. A deathbed promise is the most binding promise. You told her you would take care of her young'uns. That you wouldn't let anything happen to them. I suspect you've got some serious heart thinking to do."

The fire began to fade and lose its heat. Reminded me of Etha dying. Still and cold in her hospital bed, me holding her hand, the heat just leaving her. She was gone. Poppy stood up and put his pipe and razor away, hung the strop back up beside the hearth. "I'll blow out all the lamps but one. You take care of the one beside the door. Don't sit up too late."

"Good night, Poppy," I said and turned back to the fire for a bit longer. The house settled into its own sleep. My eyes shut for just a bit, the soft light lulling me into a sweet rest, one I hadn't felt in months. The cat's cries woke me. It sounded as though it was on the front porch pacing back and forth. I thought I heard something scratching at the door.

I stoked the fire one last time making sure all the coals were pushed back in the fireplace and the screen in place. I eased over to the bed Dinah and I shared. Her breathing was steady. The cat hadn't bothered her sleep. I tucked her a bit tighter and went to check the door. It was latched tight, no scratching. Maybe I was just hearing things in my dreams.

The cat's cries stopped as abrupt as they began. I blew out the lamp and changed into my flannel gown. Maybe tonight, I thought, maybe tonight I can sleep without dreams. Dinah never stirred when I slid under the covers. I listened for night sounds and willed my breathing to slow down.

I don't know how long she had been standing at the foot of the bed. "Lizzie," I heard her whisper. "Wake up."

I sat up in bed careful not to wake Dinah. I didn't try to speak. Walt's mother was a formidable woman in life and in death even more so. I only met her once or twice after Etha married Walt. Mrs. Weaver was a beautiful woman who lived a hard life raising kids and grandkids. A Christian woman who prayed and believed. Dead four years, she now stood at the foot of my bed. I wasn't afraid.

"Lizzie," she said. "Mrs. Abernathy from over at the John Tarleton home for orphans came and took the children. Now, Etha and Walt's baby girls are crying for their mama day after day. Night after night. The boys are trying to keep an eye on them, but they have the boys on one floor and the girls on the other. Mrs. Abernathy plans to adopt baby Wanda out to another family in the next few weeks. Walt's never going to see those babies again."

"I'm trying to raise Dinah by myself," I said. "Walt has a world of problems nobody can help."

"You made Etha a promise," she said, "a promise before God and Walt that you would take care of her babies, that you wouldn't let anything happen to them. Now the county has them, and Mrs. Abernathy said they would stay there, that no Weaver would ever lay their hands on those babies.

I reckon you only have one choice—raise those babies like you promised your sister. Walt will come to love you, maybe not the way he loved Etha or the way you love him, but you can have a good life."

The cat started crying again, louder and more distressed. Pitiful. And then Mrs. Weaver was gone. After a while, her wailing got fainter and fainter as daylight crested the ridge behind the house. Sleep never came, my head and heart at odds.

Daylight wasn't far off. I heard Mommy stir and dress. Soon, she would be at the stove beginning her day. Poppy would leave for the mines. And I would wait on the porch for Walt to come up the road and take us away.

The youngest of seven children—mine, yours, and ours—I grew up hearing about how my mama came to marry my daddy and raise her sister's four children after her sister passed away in 1937. Etha and Lizzie were close sisters. Lizzie had a daughter in 1928. Soon after, Etha married Walt. Between 1929 and 1937, they had six children. Two of those died, the last with Etha's death.

———

SUE WEAVER DUNLAP *lives in Walland, Tennessee, on a mountain farm with her husband Raymond. Publications include* Appalachian Journal, Appalachian Heritage, Pine Mountain Sand and Gravel, Anthology of Appalachian Writers, Kakalak, *and* The Southern Poetry Anthology. *Dunlap's works also include* A Walk to the Spring House, Iris Press, 2021, Knead, Main Street Rag, 2016, *and* Story Tender, Finishing Line Press, 2014.

No. — TEN —

THINGS ONLY SHE COULD SEE

Kane, Pennsylvania

———

KAREN GENTILMAN CLOPP

"Karen, your father is in trouble!"

Home from college for the summer, I was sound asleep in my bed that morning. My mother's frantic words and the urgency and fear in her usually calm voice jolted me awake.

"What's wrong?" I asked.

"I just walked into the bathroom, and when I looked down at the tub, it was filled with water," she said. "Your dad was lying completely still at the bottom with his eyes open."

"What?"

"The image only lasted a few seconds. The tub is empty now. But I saw what I saw. Something happened, and I'm worried."

I glanced at the clock. It was 7 a.m.

"Go back to sleep," I said. "Dad is working. If he's in trouble, someone will call. Everything will be fine.

I was used to my mother's "visions" and wasn't particularly concerned.

At the time, my father was working as the custodian for the local YMCA in Kane, Pennsylvania.

Later, when I went downstairs, my mother seemed fine. I asked about her early morning appearance at my bedroom door, and she said the danger had passed.

Around noon, I was in the kitchen watching my mother prepare a sandwich for my father, who always came home for lunch. I heard his car pull up. Usually, he would come directly up onto the side porch and into the kitchen. That day was different. He came on the porch, but not inside. After several minutes I went out to see if anything was wrong.

I found him emptying the contents of his wallet and laying each item on the porch railing. His driver's license and other items were drenched. Then I noticed he was wearing different clothing than he usually wore to work.

"What happened?" I asked.

"Oh, when I was testing the temperature of the water this morning at the pool, I leaned over a little too far and fell in, clothing, shoes, wallet, and all."

I asked what time that happened.

It was seven o'clock, right around the time my mother told me of her vision.

For her entire life, my mother had an unusually high level of extra sensory perception. It became stronger after a near-death experience a few weeks after I was born in 1945. This was long before "near-death" experiences were in the news, but it was a story I heard often growing up.

Home alone with a newborn and no phone, her appendix had ruptured, resulting in peritonitis. By the time she arrived at the hospital, she was critical and was rushed into surgery. After she regained consciousness, she told my father and brothers that while the surgeon was working on her she had floated out of her body, where she remained hovering above the operating table watching the surgical team work on her. After a short time, she "floated" over to a corner of the operating room and entered a small opening in the ceiling that led to a narrow tunnel.

Once inside, she began to float toward a faint light, quickly gathering more and more momentum. She was looking forward to reaching the light at the end, when suddenly, and with a sharp jolt, she came to a complete standstill.

A voice said, "You must return to your body."

She didn't want to return to that pain.

"You have a young daughter to raise," the voice said. "You must go back."

With that, she was instantly whooshed back down the tunnel and slammed back into her body.

After that she began to see things others did not. For example, she told me she could sometimes see colors radiating off people. My mother was an extremely quiet, private woman. When these things happened, they were shared only within the family; plus, I think she was a little frightened by them.

One day, after returning from a luncheon at the local senior center, she told my father she had seen a darkness hovering around the head and shoulders of the woman sitting across from her. The following day that woman died.

A week before my mother's younger sister died, my mother dreamed the two of them were walking along a sidewalk when the ground in front of them suddenly opened and swallowed her.

Also, for the rest of my mother's life, all things electrical went haywire on her. Watches gained an hour in seconds and finally watches she wore would run for a few days and then suddenly stop. Each time my father returned them to the jewelry store for repair, the jeweler told my dad the hands had turned upward to the crystals, completely stopping their movement. Eventually, she simply stopped wearing a watch.

My mother loved listening to the radio, and one of her favorite singers was country western singer Billy Ray Cyrus. It was not my kind of music, and I often told her I couldn't understand what she saw in him. I used to kid her about it. Her favorite song near the time of her death was his hit *Achy Breaky Heart*.

"How could you like that silly song?" I would ask, and we joked about it a lot.

When my mother died of a heart attack alone in her home at age eighty-nine, I received the call but was unable to get there until the following morning. The funeral director and my uncle, who had found her, assured me they had turned everything off—lights, television, radio, and washing machine—all of which had been on or running at the time of her death.

I was terribly apprehensive about entering the house. I turned the key, opened the door, and after a few seconds of complete silence, the radio in the room where she died lit up, and suddenly the entire house was filled with the deafening sound of Billy Ray Cyrus singing *Achy Breaky Heart*!

I often wondered how the radio managed to turn itself on and play that exact song just moments after I entered the room. It was not plugged into the wall outlet, and it did not have a battery. Was it merely a remaining spark of electricity residing inside the unit, or was it caused by my mother's remaining energy in that room?

A few months after her death, I was sound asleep in the middle of the night when I was awakened by a slight movement at the bottom of the bed. The bedroom was faintly lit by a nightlight from the adjoining hall. When

I opened my eyes, I was shocked to see a figure standing upright at the foot of the bed. I could clearly see it was an image of a short, elderly woman, dressed in a loose-fitting coat or robe with a shawl pulled over the top of her head. It was slightly blurry, yet seemed to be three-dimensional.

Alarmed, I jumped out of bed. As I began to move toward the figure, it quickly dissipated. This apparition frightened me. I remained awake for a long time afterwards with the kind of chills that run up a person's spine and exit the top of their head. I sometimes still get those exact same chills in her house. It has happened several times in her kitchen when I find myself thinking of her. It makes me wonder if some of her unusually strong energy is still alive in that house.

I have also often thought about the woman standing at the foot of my bed. Was it a specter sent by my mother, or was it her spirit ghost paying one last visit to her only daughter before departing this earth forever?

I have chosen to believe it was her because some things simply cannot be explained by reason or empirical observation. I saw what I saw, and I heard what I heard. To quote Hamlet's words from Shakespeare's play, "There are more things in heaven and earth, Horatio, than are dreamt of in your philosophy."

———

KAREN GENTILMAN CLOPP *was born and raised in Kane, Pennsylvania. Her mother, Minnie, was a coal miner's daughter who was blessed (or cursed) with a heightened sense of extra sensory perception. Growing up, the "visions" her mother experienced gave Karen a sense of wonder as she imagined a world beyond the visible one. She enjoys playing a variety of musical instruments. Since retiring, Karen has played fiddle with various old time and Celtic musical groups in Western New York and Western Pennsylvania. She enjoys photographing the wildlife and wildflowers that surround her home, which is just north of Allegany State Park.*

— ELEVEN —

WITH GHOSTS, SWEARING HELPS

Williamson County, Tennessee

———

JUDITH DUVALL

A friend bought an old mansion set on rolling fields and edged by beautiful, mature trees and invited me to stay with her any time I was in the area. I enjoyed going there not only to be with my friend but also to enjoy such a gorgeous, rambling place. It was full of history and was famous for having served as a hospital for wounded soldiers during the Civil War. The local historical society had scads of documentation displayed at a museum and often hinted that my friend should sponsor tours for the public. That wasn't going to happen because she had moved to the country to get away from her frantic city job.

On my visits, we spent a lot of time in the kitchen and the adjacent room she dubbed the family room. That's where we often enjoyed our dinner, using TV trays and watching television. The fun started on my very first visit. We were tuned to the news and stuffing our faces when the lights began to flicker. Mind you, not the television or the lights in the kitchen, only the lights in the family room.

"The damn place is haunted," she explained.

She said the flickering lights, noises in empty rooms, doors slamming, and her kitchen radio suddenly blaring occurred often when she was alone, but never when others were around. She was surprised "they acted up" when I was present. I had no idea what it meant, but my friend thought the "ghost" felt threatened by me. I had a big laugh over that idea and asked her who she thought was messing with the lights.

After explaining the story of the house being used as a Civil War hospital and the many men who died there, I began to see that a few restless souls might not be happy hanging around a place that held unpleasant memories. I suggested that my friend might want to speak to the invisible visitors and suggest they leave. We had both heard stories of people telling dying loved ones to "go to the light" and we thought that might work. My friend agreed it was worth a try, but nothing else along the lines of spookiness occurred during my stay.

I visited many times over a period of two years and witnessed more of the flickering lights. Once when we were treating ourselves to a special dinner in the huge dining room the chandelier began to shake so violently we worried the crystal pieces might break. When all was quiet again, I wisecracked that someone had expected an invitation to our dinner. After all, these beings evidently felt quite at home now. My friend gave me a long look and spouted some serious swear words ending with "You're probably right."

I always stayed in the same upstairs room at the front of the house. The large four-poster bed, dresser, chest, and rocking chair were antiques bought specifically for the room. The view from two large windows framed stately oak trees and a well-kept lawn. I loved the room, especially since the door to the bathroom was only a few steps away.

On the very same night of the shaky chandelier, I woke up needing to use the bathroom. I turned on the lamp next to the bed, and it immediately began to flicker. I waited a second to see if it would stop, but it kept flickering, then went out. I turned the switch several times and nothing happened.

"I've had enough of your fucking around," I shouted. "Stop messing with the lights and get the hell outta here!"

The lamp came on.

I went to the bathroom, muttering to myself about creepy old houses and freaks obsessed with electricity.

When I crawled back into bed, I gave another shout-out into the dark room, "You'd better not bother me again, dumbass!"

That worked. When I woke the next morning my robe was on the floor, but I wasn't sure I hadn't dropped it myself.

At breakfast my friend told me she heard me shouting and, chuckling a bit, said my tone scared her more than the ghost ever had. I laughed with her and told her I was now sure of one thing: The ghost could hear when spoken to directly and, knowing that, she should begin talking them out of her house.

I didn't visit again for several months. When I did, I learned she had consulted a Native American shaman about her ghost problem. The shaman came to the house and performed several ceremonies, burned a lot of sage, said more than one "spirit" was trapped there and left with the advice, "If they come back, try telling them to leave."

She did. She didn't wait for the lights to flicker, a door to slam or any other annoying trick. Remembering how my angry shout had worked, she decided that loud, firm language would be most effective. She also thought if these were spirits of dead soldiers, a few swear words would get the message across. So every time she thought of it, she told them to get the hell out of her house.

Within a year all the spook stuff stopped. When I last visited her in that lovely old house, it was winter, and we were enjoying mulled wine and a lively fire as we chatted and caught up on our lives. Nothing disturbed our evening together and as I turned toward the stairs for bed, I asked her about the ghosts.

"Yeah, they're gone," she said. "I yelled and shouted and swore them out of here. But you know what? Sometimes I actually miss them."

———

JUDITH DUVALL*'s poems and fiction have been published by Greyhound Books, Tellico Books, Kudzu Literary Anthology,* Motif, The Tennessee Magazine, *and anthologies published by The Knoxville Writers' Guild and others. Her book of poetry,* Unrationed Hope, *was published by Iris Press. She attributes much of her writing success to the support of fellow members of the Knoxville Writers' Guild. After years of moving around the USA and other countries, she now lives, dreams, and writes near English Mountain and Douglas Lake in Jefferson County, Tennessee.*

THE GHOSTS ON SKYLINE DRIVE
Ashland, Kentucky

———

GREER LITTON FOX

Skyline Drive today is one of many once-rural roadways
that still follow the rolling contours of the Appalachians.
It's lined with drive-ins and telephone poles, gas stations,
and convenience stores. Once-pastured hillsides are
scattered with suburban houses. You can still find overlooks
that offer a now-largely-obscured view of the city of
Ashland, Kentucky. But there's no talk anymore of ghosts
or gunshots or screams in the night, no speculation of
hauntings or revenge, no stories of encounters with a wild-
eyed girl, bleeding from her face and waving blood-soaked
hands, threatening young couples, and warning them away.

No talk of the murders that effectively ended an era for this once-vibrant city. Yet some of us remember. Some of us never left. Some of us who no longer live there know what happened. We know these ghosts. The ghosts are real.

Ashland, Kentucky, has been in decline since before the turn of the twenty-first century, its population a mere whisper of what it was in the years following the Second World War. Jobs by the thousands have disappeared as the large corporations began, one by one, to leave the area. But Ashland was in its prime in the early 1960s. Good jobs were plentiful; Ashland was home to Armco Steel, Ashland Oil & Refining Company, a busy tannery, several banks, law firms, even a community college. Downtown churches of many denominations drew large congregations able to support stately buildings. The Hotel Henry Clay, Parsons Department Store, the Paramount Theater, and not one, but three "five and dimes" were among the landmarks in a vibrant downtown. Public parks hosted baseball teams for boys of all ages, the high school basketball team had become a powerhouse across the state, and civic groups of all sorts pulled the community together.

The city fathers coined the motto: "Ashland—a busy, friendly city." And it was, for many. Prosperity made it easy to overlook the rundown homes, shacks by any standard, that dotted the outskirts around town and were tucked away at the bottom of steep hills inside the city. Even then, some youngsters grew up in areas where streets had no curbs, trash was everywhere, cars were junked and left in front yards, and children were on their own, often truant, often hungry.

Skyline Drive in the 1960s was a peaceful, lightly traveled country roadway that paralleled U.S. Route 60, the main highway into Ashland. From the pullouts—many with picnic tables—along the top of Skyline Drive where the trees had been cut back you could see all the way past the city and across the Ohio River to the rocky bluffs of Ohio. It was a favorite route for families whose main entertainment on Sunday afternoons was a drive into the country to see the scenery. At night, you could see the lights of the bustling city. Among teenagers, Skyline Drive was known for one thing only: It was a prime make-out place. Even "nice girls" went there. At night, teenagers owned "the Drive." Rumors of ghosts, of midnight hauntings had yet to be whispered.

The Ashland High School senior class was in high spirits in March 1962. Our boys had just won the state basketball championship and parades, pep rallies, and honors banquets kept us entertained while we made plans for our futures after graduation, just a short two months away. Jobs, marriage, college, freedom—a wealth of possibility dominated our thoughts and conversations. Nothing could have prepared us for the collective nightmare we were about to experience.

Our first awareness of tragedy was during second period: Screams and crying—the desperate, keening sounds of inconsolable mourning—reverberated through the hallways of the high school and silenced all classroom talk. Our teacher went out to see what was going on and came back with a stricken look on her face. She said nothing for a moment, seeming to wage an internal war between telling us what she'd learned and sheltering us for a few moments more of innocence.

There was no going back, no denial possible of what we would learn. Mary Jean Carter and her boyfriend had been murdered the night before, and their bodies had just been found on Skyline Drive. Mary Jean's best friends were hysterical. Parents were called to take them home. As word spread, the anguish and grief spread. Senior classes were dismissed for the day.

Mary Jean was a classmate of mine from first grade to our senior year. Even in first grade, she was a beauty: long, glossy brown hair she wore in curls, large bright brown eyes with thick lashes, a sweet face, and such a spirit! She talked, she laughed, she was tough, she was popular.

At the beginning of our senior year, Mary Jean was dating a boy—a man, really—from Ceredo, Ohio, a town just a little way across the Ohio River and down toward South Point. Larry Wainwright was his name. He had already finished high school and had a job. He even had a car of his own. We were impressed. Mary Jean loved showing him off. He was older than we were, and his good looks matched hers. They made a striking couple.

And they were a couple. Mary Jean's best friends confessed to her parents that Mary Jean and Larry had gotten married secretly and were planning to tell both sets of parents just as soon as Mary Jean received her high school diploma. It is not surprising that Mary Jean and Larry were on Skyline Drive that night. Skyline Drive offered what nowhere else could: privacy for them to be alone together, in love, in a beautiful setting. What Skyline Drive did not offer was safety.

When the coroner announced that the autopsy showed Mary Jean was two months pregnant, a renewed cascade of grief and horror and loss spread throughout the city and again felled both sets of families. The city was on edge for months while the police investigated all leads. Finally, two defendants were identified—Artie Rice and Earl Caudill—twenty-year-olds who had graduated from Ashland High two years earlier. They had been in my sister's class. We all knew them. You can find pictures of all three of them—Mary Jean, Artie, and Earl—frozen now forever, in the pages of the 1960 Ashland High School Annual.

At the trial, two witnesses testified they saw Larry's car parked at one of the pull-outs and a second car that belonged to Artie Rice parked not far away. Artie and his co-defendant, Earl Caudill, were armed with a gun and knives when they approached Larry's car. First, they shot and fatally wounded Larry and then attacked and raped Mary Jean. The coroner's report showed that Mary Jean was still alive when she was found the next morning... still alive, despite a bullet in her brain, stab wounds in her face and breast, her hands mutilated by the knife blade, all evidence of how valiantly she fought with the two killers.

The coroner described a mighty struggle, such that she still attempted to fight them off after they stabbed her in the chest—which broke her sternum—and then they shot her in the head.

A neighbor testified that earlier that day she had watched from her porch as Mary Jean crossed the street to avoid the heckling and catcalls Artie and Earl were hurling at her. This was the early 1960s, when any man could view any woman as fair game with impunity. Was their motive retribution for rejection? The prosecutor speculated as much. He pointed out that robbery was not their aim, as they had left untouched "a considerable amount of money" found in Larry's car. Artie was described by one of his classmates as "uglier than homemade sin." Was Mary Jean made to pay for Artie's lifetime of insults and slurs?

Both Artie and Earl were sentenced to life in prison, a sentence reconfirmed after Artie appealed the guilty verdict in 1966 on grounds that the bullet removed from Mary Jean's brain tissue was so mutilated it could not be positively identified as having come from Artie's gun. The Appellate Court denied his appeal and reaffirmed his sentence.

In the months that followed the discovery of the murders, Skyline Drive was deserted except for the frequent patrols of the city police and the daytime drive-bys of the curious, drawn by lurid interest in seeing for themselves the scene of the crime. And yet, reports of strange noises—especially when the winds blew through the trees—circulated throughout the county, rumors whispered and pooh-poohed at church suppers and in classrooms, wherever people gathered to talk. Soon enough, family cars began to return on Sunday afternoons and young couples began to drift back to the highline pullouts for the same reasons Mary Jean and Larry went there.

If you go now—some sixty years later—to Skyline Drive, you will find no tangible evidence of these murders. The crosses and memorials placed there immediately after the discovery of their deaths have since disappeared. Trash and debris litter the pullouts at the top of the road. Only the trees and weeds remain, still cut back a bit to showcase the views of the town, now seedy and ravaged by joblessness and drugs, and the river beyond. But if you get out of your car, stand, and listen awhile, you will hear the cry of an unborn child and the soft voices of its parents as they murmur sweet words of love.

———

Following a career as a UTK Distinguished Professor, **GREER LITTON FOX** *enrolled in a workshop at the Aspen Institute's Summer Words program. Her first story won a Knoxville Writers' Guild prize for narrative nonfiction. Subsequent stories and poems have appeared in the* Avocet *and various anthologies. The inspiration for "The Ghosts of Skyline Drive" was a writing prompt—loss of a classmate—offered by a guest speaker at a meeting of the Poetry Society of Tennessee. It honors the brief life of a high school classmate. Greer is currently writing a children's book about the adventures of two coyote brothers.*

— THIRTEEN —

A HAUNTING WOVEN THROUGH GRIEF

Kingsport, Tennessee

BRAD LIFFORD

The Kingsport farmhouse was stately and situated on rich bottomland near a creek, expansive with thirteen rooms, and it bore a magical name. Mary Birdwell and Carole Carroll, sisters, can vividly describe the wonders of growing up in the 1940s and '50s in the house called Roseland.

The great kitchen had a massive hearth for cooking, and every room was heated by a fireplace. In winter, that wasn't enough.

"You had to have a stack of blankets to stay warm," Mary remembers.

There were also mysteries.

On winter nights, had they been able to stay awake through the dead of night, the girls would have experienced a strange sensation. The feeling of one quilt in particular, red and made of rough fabric, that crept down the length of the bed, pulled by unseen fingers toward the foot. This invisible grasp was determined to liberate the red quilt and drag it to the floor—whether it was on top of the stack, in the middle, or weighted down at the bottom.

The red quilt belonged to Amanda Ellen Steadman, a master weaver and quiltmaker who lived at Roseland until her death in 1939 and, many believe, was so grief-stricken she never left the home.

The girls were too young to form any memories of their great-aunt, but Mary and Carole knew "Aunt El" anyway. It was not only the restless quilt that left an impression.

Reflecting on those memories today Carole points to a large glass globe lamp in Mary's living room. "Sometimes we would hear the sound of glass breaking, like from a lamp that size," she says, "and we would go try to find what made that sound. We never could find any broken glass."

Roseland, which dated to the late 18th century, had an organ room, or parlor room. Sometimes, the Shipp family—Mary and Carole had two sisters, Margaret and Helen—played music on the pump organ. Other times, they heard music from the organ when no player was on the bench. Roseland was graced with other mysterious music. A closet in the great kitchen was home to an accordion and sometimes the family would hear accordion music—even when no hands were squeezing the instrument.

The Shipp parents were familiar with Aunt El's presence. The mother sometimes felt as if she were being watched by someone or something unseen—the feeling would raise the hairs on her neck. Carole would sew at a sewing station outside her father's bedroom on the second floor, where there was no nearby window. "I could sometimes feel a breeze at my neck, but I just learned to accept it," she says.

Aunt El was not generally a happy person, their mother told them. In two black-and-white photos, Ellen Steadman wears a severe expression. Ellen was pierced with heartbreak at least once. She never married and never had children. Stories handed down through the family indicate she didn't generally warm to children—but Aunt El did have a special niece.

That niece, Mary Lee, died mysteriously at age five. The exact cause of her death is lost to the passage of time, but there is consensus that it centered around an apple butter stir, a common rite of autumn on the farm. The child was helping with the stir, and the story goes that she licked the stirring paddle clean after the apple butter was done, developed an infection, and died.

Aunt El was despondent. She could not sleep for three days. She could not bear the thought of her young niece being buried without some sort of ceremonial covering handmade by her aunt. The woman quickly made a funeral coverlet, flowers woven into the fabric, to wrap around the small coffin.

Atop a hill not far from that original location of Roseland, a family cemetery includes many graves of those who passed away through the decades—including Aunt El and her special niece.

The Roseland of today rests elsewhere in Kingsport. When they were grown with families of their own, and their father and then their mother were gone, the Shipp daughters decided to donate Roseland to a Kingsport living history museum.

When crews disassembled the cabin, they discovered it was actually three cabins pieced together over time. The house was resurrected a few miles away at Exchange Place and, in 1990, was dedicated to the Shipp family, as well as the Steadman and Bachman families that preceded in ownership dating back 200 years. The ancient hand-hewn logs and ornate porch molding and antiques were not all that made their way to the new resting place.

"Oh, Aunt El is with Roseland, there's no doubt about it," Mary says.

Exchange Place volunteers have reported lights coming on and turning off when no one is inside. Doors slam by themselves. One longtime volunteer, Heather Gilreath, got locked into the attic when the stairwell door she entered closed and locked after she had ascended the stairs. Fortunately, she was able to scrabble over a low log wall and descend another spiral staircase.

She and other volunteers accept that Aunt El is responsible for such benign occurrences. And Mark Selby, a Steadman descendant, is among the volunteer workers who, when they enter Roseland, offer a greeting just in case: "Hello, Aunt El. It's just me."

As for Mary and Carole, they remember those formative days. They have possession of a storage trunk that includes personal possessions of Aunt El, including a love letter from a beau seeking her hand. What they have not found is an old funeral dress from Roseland that went missing when they were kids. Nor do they know what happened to the red quilt. And Mary isn't sure she would claim it if she did.

"I would be leery of that quilt, I think," she says.

———

A cofounder of Howling Hills, **BRAD LIFFORD** *is a writer and editor who lives in Kingsport, Tennessee, with his wife, Tammy. He is the coauthor of* East Tennessee Garden Stories *and is at work on* The Good Pint Trail: A Guide to East Tennessee Breweries.

Getting my Mojo back

Johnson City, Tennessee

DANIEL PEACOCK

I'm not sure what led my parents to adopt a miniature
dachshund for us when we were in grade school. Mojo
had to have been the only wiener-dog in the entire county.
He was the most majestic thing my sister and I had seen,
a purebred cylinder of German-engineered cuddles. He
would greet us every day when we came home from school,
running up to us as fast as his tiny legs could take him.
He had a specific way of wagging his tail when he saw us
that set the whole back half of his body wagging as well. It
looked like he was shaking his hips.

We fell in love with his tiny little legs, too small to take him upstairs in a straight line. Instead, he would shimmy up one end of his long body onto a step, then the other. It looked like a slinky going in reverse. We loved the odd thumping sound he made when he ran, accompanied by the metallic jangle of his collar. He had to be the most unusual dog our friends and family had ever seen, a creature that seemed to belong in some rich person's parlor. Instead, he was out rolling in mud and the clay with us country bumpkins in rural Georgia.

Like any good country dog, he lived both inside and outside the house. We tried to teach Mojo that the outside was for playing and pooping, but he preferred the indoors for both. He could be what we called *ornery*, bearing a sour temperament with a hint of mischief. And he could hide a pile of poo like it was gold. We would catch a whiff in the living room and spend the next thirty minutes hunting beneath the furniture for it. We had a pool, and if you were sitting on an inflatable life raft and drifted too close to the edge, Mojo would bite a hole through the plastic and shuffle away as you deflated into the water. But the worst of his vices was chasing cars.

Our house had a massive front yard that sloped up to the road. Once Mojo was old enough to think he was ten feet tall, he began racing up that yard any time a car passed by. He would pursue each one with purpose, barking until the car rounded the corner like he was chasing off a threat. We knew this was a recipe for disaster, so we started trying everything to keep him from chasing cars. We stopped letting him out on his own; we got a leash for him; we even started putting a bright orange parka on him in the winter.

One fateful day, Mojo was hit by a passing truck as we were leaving for a 4-H meeting in town. Pa carried him from the road, and we all helped bury him beneath a walnut tree. In a cruel twist, I had been chosen that next day to recite the preamble to the Constitution to classes throughout my school. I pulled it off, but not without sob breaks between classrooms.

In time, the loss of Mojo turned from a sharp pain to a dull ache. Fourth-grade Daniel had never experienced anything like this, and I still had days where the thought of him put me in a foul mood.

One night, I awoke around four o'clock in the morning to use the bathroom. My bedroom was at the end of a long hallway, with the bathroom at the opposite end. I dragged myself through the darkness, feeling along the wall for the light switch. My eyes adjusted a little to the darkness before I could find the switch, and I noticed a small shape in the living room. I froze, straining my eyes to make out what it was.

Something living crouched on the floor. I couldn't shake the feeling it was looking back at me. I began to worry that a rabid cat had climbed into our house. As I stared, another feeling crept in. Comfort. Something about this shape crouched before me seemed benevolent. More than anything, it felt curious about me. As this feeling washed over me, I spoke aloud the first thing that came to my mind.

"Mojo?"

The shape seemed to rise a little and start wiggling. Not the whole shape, mind you, just its back half. It stayed a moment, wiggling in what felt like joy to me, then bound away deeper into the darkness without a sound—except for the soft jangle of a metal collar.

Once I found the light switch, the living room was empty. I raised such a fuss looking for whatever I had seen that my dad came trudging down the stairs with a shotgun, expecting to find a robbery in progress.

I still can't say for certain what I saw. Maybe I craved closure over losing Mojo so abruptly that my young mind turned a strange shadow into my dead dog. It felt too real to dismiss so easily, but I'm nothing if not a skeptical guy. That said, part of me will always know that it was Mojo, taking a break from chasing cars in the dog afterlife, excited to greet me one last time.

———

DANIEL PEACOCK *of Johnson City first traveled to Northeast Tennessee to attend college. These days, he spends his time "nerding out" about everything from history and hiking to films and video games. He and his wife, Kennedy, live with an ornery cat named Totoro.*

No.

— FIFTEEN —

THE LOST VALLEY OF HARDIN

Hardin Valley, Tennessee

LAURA STILL

By the time I first visited, Hardin Valley was already gone, turned into a congested interstate exit, where the main campus of Pellissippi State Community College maintained borders crowded with apartment and housing developments, trade and business "parks," and shopping centers. I detested going there because of the traffic and my sadness over the few remnants of what must have been lovely green fields and groves of trees before suburban sprawl took over.

When asked to speak on campus after the publication of my book *A Haunted History of Knoxville*, I was reluctant, and not just because of the twenty-mile drive. They wanted me to talk about why the campus was haunted. How could there be ghosts? The school had only been here since 1986. The buildings looked sturdy and convenient, but not at all spooky. Why would they hint that something was wrong with certain buildings, that students were uncomfortable, even frightened inside them? There were also reports of shadowy figures appearing at night just out of range of the outdoor lights. It didn't feel possible, but if enough people were talking, maybe something was connected to the place itself. I began to research Hardin Valley history to see what spirits might be stirring in the dark hours of night—or day, for that matter.

Hardin Valley was named for Colonel Joseph Hardin, a Revolutionary War veteran who was given a land grant of 6,000 acres in this area in 1795. Hardin moved here shortly after, bringing his wife and twelve children. The colonel built his home and a blockhouse along the Buttermilk Trail, named for the springs and later the springhouses along the road where early settlers made and sold buttermilk. (Much later it was renamed Hardin Valley Road.) The blockhouse was necessary because of the ever-present danger of violence between the settlers and the Native Americans they came to displace.

A few remnants of the Creek and Choctaw remained, but the Cherokee were the main indigenous people in this area when European settlers began to venture in after the Revolutionary War. The Cherokee had built a series of towns along a part of the Holston River that was renamed the Tennessee in 1890. These lands were considered sacred, and they were ready to fight and die for them.

There is a family story of two Hardin sons leaving to take a herd of cattle to Nashville. Mrs. Hardin bid them good-bye and asked the oldest to take care of himself and his brother. She was expecting a baby, and the eldest brother asked that, if he didn't make it back, the baby be named after him. On the way to market, the Cherokees attacked, and he was killed. The younger brother was captured and kept prisoner. The family gave up both for dead and named the new baby after the oldest brother. Three years later, the Cherokee brought the younger brother to the family and offered to sell him back. The Hardins ransomed him for six horses. The young man always claimed his dead brother protected him and saved his life. Later descendants said the spirit of the murdered young man appeared whenever a family member was in danger. Could he be one of the shades guarding the campus grounds?

The Hardin children grew up and married. Some moved farther west into the new territories that opened up after the removal of the native tribes. Other Hardins scattered around the valley, dividing the original land grant into family farms. One descendant, Barbara Keith Taylor, had two sons who fought in the Civil War, on opposite sides. George joined the Union troops and was sent north to Kentucky. He was later shot by a spy and brought home to the Knoxville Hospital, where his mother could see him before he died.

Samuel, much to his mother's distress, joined the Confederate Army. She blamed her cousins for this and said the Jones boys lured him to the Rebel side. When Sam came marching through Knoxville, she refused to see him. Later, a relation brought the news that he was killed at Chickamauga. He had been suffering from yellow fever, but Sam refused his captain's permission to go on sick leave. His body was buried with hundreds of others in an unmarked grave near the battlefield. The South's bloody victory had turned hollow by the time his mother learned of his death. General Braxton Bragg refused to pursue the Northern troops after the battle, enabling them to escape and recuperate, while the Confederate troops never recovered from the loss of twenty percent of their fighting force.

Barbara may have mourned her son but didn't speak of it. Instead, she continued her feud with those she blamed for corrupting him, the Jones boys. Confederate troops broke into her barn and stole livestock after the nearby battle of Campbell's Station, and she blamed her cousins for leading them to her farm. After the war she refused to have dealings with the Jones boys, calling them wild and untrustworthy, and not worth shooting. Late in her life she continued to insist it was their fault she never saw her son again.

Or did she? If ever a ghost had reason to walk, it would be Sam Taylor's, who died without a last good-bye or a kind word from his mother. Did he come back to haunt his old home after the war? Stories of Rebel ghosts are common in Hardin Valley, and Sam could be among them. His mother's house and barn disappeared long ago, but his spirit may roam the road and fields looking for the place, hoping to find peace and forgiveness at last. It might explain the somber shadow reported to follow an occasional student leaving a night class.

If Sam wanders campus, he may have company, for the feud with the Jones boys had one more victim. Barbara Taylor's second husband was James Doughty and their only child was Parallee, born in 1858. Parallee grew up to marry and had children of her own. The oldest boy was named Homer and liked to hunt. One day he went out with some of the Jones cousins and never came back. The Jones boys said they were climbing a fence when one of their guns went off. Wasn't it odd that the bullet should end up killing Homer, the oldest grandson of Barbara Taylor? Parallee and her husband never pressed charges, but none of their sons were allowed to go hunting again. Those Jones boys were a little too accident prone. Young Homer's tragic spirit cast a shadow over the rest of his siblings, and maybe he and his Uncle Sam meet up on campus to compare notes about those troublesome Jones boys.

After the war, the remaining Hardin Valley families had to work hard to make ends meet, and some of the next generations moved away from the land, since the farms weren't big enough to give all of them a living. Their best cash crop was whiskey. Moonshine runners brought it by wagon and later by truck to the Gallaher Ferry on the Clinch River, then stashed the liquor at prearranged hiding places on the Knox County side. The bootleggers would then come to pick it up and distribute it to thirsty customers. This continued through Prohibition and into the Depression. Though there was no work and crops were poor, a market for whiskey could always be found. Occasional feuds among rival moonshiners and periodic raids by revenue men brought accompanying gunfire and mayhem. Restless spirits of those times are said to linger, and older residents would tell tales of seeing lights and hearing sounds of revving engines in the hills and hollers, as the shades of old moonshiners revisited the scenes of dangerous chases in the night.

The TVA came into the valley in 1936 to help farmers with soil erosion, encourage new agricultural techniques, and provide free fertilizer. Hardin Valley began to experience a period of prosperity and growth. Oak Ridge arrived during the World War II years and brought an influx of workers and new residents. The Hardin Valley School, built in 1890, was enlarged and improved. New churches and homes were also built for the growing population, but Hardin Valley remained primarily rural. In 1978, the school burned down and students were transferred to Karns and Solway. The community protested, but no funding for a new school could be found.

In 1982, a Metropolitan Planning Commission staff planner was interviewed by a Knoxville paper and explained the

Hardin Valley area had remained rural for one reason: a lack of basic public services, such as sewers, and roadways. "Without better services," he said, "it is unlikely that anything would change much."

Four years later, Pellissippi State Community College had been built, and a sewer line laid for the campus, which could be extended beyond the college. Suddenly developers had dollar signs in their eyes. Suburbs began springing up all over the valley. Instead of the sound of cows and chickens the roar of backhoes and bulldozers split the air as they dug up the fields. The college had unintentionally been the catalyst for the destruction of a way of life that had lasted almost two hundred years.

Though the early settlers and old families of the valley would never recognize it today, the land that they took from the Cherokees is still underneath the skin of asphalt and concrete we have given it. The native peoples were eventually conquered and carried away, though some say they left guardian spirits over the lands that had been theirs. Would they still be lingering after all this time? Perhaps. And maybe the souls of all those who replaced the Cherokee understand the feelings of the First People now, and their love for their lost valley causes their spirits to return.

When a new Hardin Valley school was finally approved and building begun, the bell from the old 1890 school, the only thing saved from the fire that destroyed it, was installed. Generations of children had grown up being summoned to class by that bell. Perhaps it summons them now to awaken and protest the destruction of the land that sustained them—I wouldn't be surprised.

———

Native East Tennessean **LAURA STILL** *is a published poet, playwright, and local history author. She created Knoxville Walking Tours in 2012 and works full-time as a storyteller and walking history guide. She has researched and written fifteen tours, including three ghost walks. She partners with the Knoxville History Project and proceeds from her tours support it and other history-oriented Knoxville nonprofits. Co-owner of Celtic Cat Publishing since 2016, she has written four books:* Guardians (2009), Acts of the Apostles, Vol. 1, (2010), A Haunted History of Knoxville (2014), *and* A Fair Shake: The Leaders of the Fight for Women's Rights in Knoxville (2021).

No.

— SIXTEEN —

NOT OUR EXIT
Dunlap, Tennessee

———

NATALIE KIMBELL

I was driving home to Fredonia Mountain with my seven-year-old daughter after shopping for school clothes and supplies in Chattanooga. My thirteen-year-old son Nathan had convinced me he was old enough to stay home alone, and I was in a hurry to get back. I was thankful we were traveling on Tennessee State Highway 111, which was fairly new, and not Highway 127, where The World's Longest Yard Sale was taking place for the twelfth year. The yard sale stretched hundreds of miles across four states, attracting bargain hunters from all over the nation. Thousands of people would be dotting the two-lane highway looking for everything from antiques to clothing. Thankfully, I would skirt most of the crowd, though vendors would be huddled at the four-way intersection in Dunlap.

We still had three miles to go before getting off the highway when my daughter surprised me.

"Momma, this is our exit," Tricia insisted from the back seat.

She was so concerned I slowed down to point out landmarks to show her she was mistaken. "No honey, that's the way to the East Valley Road. We don't live in that direction."

"But Momma, we need to turn!" she urged.

She was visibly upset. I had no idea why and slowed down even more. I considered going that way just to calm her, knowing that meandering along farmland backroads would add ten minutes or more to our trip. But I wanted to get back. My son had been left alone long enough, so I drove on.

On that particular day—August 14, 1998—the sky was clear and sunny. The view from Lewis Chapel Mountain descending into the valley was spectacular, with a panoramic view of not only the sky, but miles of the Cumberland plateau and the valley floor. Deciduous and evergreen trees blanketed the hillsides. As we passed the East Valley Road exit, I glanced at my daughter in the rearview mirror. She was looking backward. She may have said something like "we missed our chance," but time has made that part of the conversation vague.

However, when we arrived at the intersection with Highway 127, I faced something I never expected— something we had missed by only a few moments. An eighteen-wheeler had plowed into the throng by the side of the road on my left. The scene was cataclysmic. A Ford sedan that had been hit by the truck was blazing, totally engulfed in flames. One man had been run over by the truck. Reports would tell of tire marks across his shirt. People were scattered, some trying to help, others in shock. Clothing that had once been for sale carpeted the road. Books were crushed and thrown from a table.

As I recount these events I feel very numb, very distant from something that should shudder me with emotion. All I can remember feeling is the immediate need to get my daughter out of there and get to my son. I was useless to those at the accident. Sirens were close, so the first opportunity I had, I continued on Highway 111 until I could cross to Fredonia Road to home. I would later learn the eighteen-wheeler's brakes had failed and that two people died in the burning car. More than twenty were injured in the accident. The man who had been run over miraculously survived.

Eventually, the four-way intersection between Highways 111 and 127 was replaced with an overpass. The World's Longest Yard Sale continues each year during the first full week of August, now stretching to six states. My daughter, now in her thirties, only vaguely remembers the accident. She remembers wanting to get off at that earlier exit but doesn't remember why. I get a chill thinking about it, knowing how close we were to being there when the accident took place, and about the lives that were lost and changed. But it's the memory of her voice from the back seat pleading with me to leave the highway before the intersection that makes the hairs on my neck stand.

———

NATALIE KIMBELL *was born in Norton, Virginia, lived for eight years in Worcester, Massachusetts, and grew up in East Tennessee. She has spent forty years teaching at her alma mater, Sequatchie County High School. She is a mother, grandmother, and writer. Her work has appeared in* Pine Mountain Sand and Gravel, Mildred Haun Review, Anthology of Appalachian Writers: Kingsolver Edition, Tennessee Voices, *and* Artemis. *Her first poetry chapbook,* On Phillips Creek, *will be published by Finishing Line Press in 2024.*

— SEVENTEEN —

THINK YOU CAN SELL
A HAUNTED HOUSE?

Knoxville, Tennessee

———

SUZY TROTTA

There are two kinds of people in this world: those who don't believe in ghosts and real estate agents. Go in and out of enough houses and you'll encounter things: footsteps up a back staircase, a feeling of being watched, a sudden smell of perfume. That might sound crazy or spooky, but you get the sense they mean you no harm.

What if you didn't get that sense? I found out one fall in the suburbs of Knoxville.

Mary called me to list a home in a very nice mid-century neighborhood. The house was her dream home, and the plan had been to live in it forever, but her husband got a job out west and she needed to sell. From the street, it was unremarkable: a mock Tudor on a fairly small, if level, lot. It was a good neighborhood and as a new agent, I was willing to list or sell anything if it meant making money.

I met her there one weekday afternoon. Mary was a large woman, tall and broad shouldered, with frizzy red hair and what today might be called a "woo woo coastal grandma" fashion sense. Turned out she lived in another home in the neighborhood and bought this one when it came up for foreclosure auction because, as mentioned, it had always been her dream home.

Looking around, I could see her dreams were not like most peoples'. The house was dark, with faux beamed ceilings. It did have nice hardwood floors, but the trim and finishes were cheap and uninspiring. There was an upstairs, but Mary was not interested in showing me that. Mary had saved the best for second to last.

Walking through a back den, we came through a door into one of the largest kitchens I have ever been in. Natural light poured through skylights in a vaulted ceiling, highlighting many linear feet of granite countertops and thousands of dollars of custom cabinetry. Not Architectural Digest material, but impressive.

Looking past the enormous kitchen island and eat-in kitchen bar, I saw two very large glass sliding doors that met in the middle. I assumed these led to the backyard, though whatever was behind them was dark, which made no sense, as it was a nice, sunny day.

"And here," she intoned like a game show host, "is the piece *de resistance*!" With a flourish, she opened the glass doors and flipped on a light, making the mysterious space visible. Beyond those doors was a pool. An indoor pool. It had the vaulted ceiling of the kitchen and even more skylights. A fountain tinkled, spa-like, in the corner between two lounge chairs. It was cozy and warm, with steam coming off the water's surface.

Then she showed me a sauna and a bathroom with a gym-like shower and changing room.

"This is why I fell in love with this house!" she exclaimed, spreading her arms out to specify *this*. I mean, it was pretty cool, but I have to be honest, it wasn't that cool. Everything was dated to the 1990s and the pool room had completely taken the place of any backyard the home once had.

"Wow!" I said, which is always a good thing to say in real estate when you don't know what else to say. Looking around, I noticed an odd metal contraption on the side of the pool that looked like it had a harness attached. "What's that?" I asked

A winch to raise and lower a person out of the pool.

She said the family that had originally lived in the house were hit by a drunk driver one night, killing the father and leaving the mother in a wheelchair. Rumors of the son's mental instability abounded before the accident, but his emotional state supposedly became precarious after the wreck.

With a sizable insurance settlement, the wife renovated the kitchen and some of the house to be nicer and wheelchair accessible. And because she still suffered pain from the accident, she built the pool and sauna for physical therapy.

According to Mary, mother and son continued to live together in the house, both deteriorating mentally and physically until the mother finally died. The son, who had never worked, squirreled himself up in the house, becoming paranoid and more delusional. He eventually hanged himself in the kitchen. Allegedly. Right where we were standing.

I should pause here to reiterate that new, broke agents will do things for money that would make a hooker blush.

Mary then told me she had worked for the Army Psychological Operations during the Vietnam War and could read people incredibly well. This was how she knew her last agent had been sneaking into the house to have sex. She was so convinced she had put tape marks on the floor by the bed posts to see if they moved from day to day. She also told me I could not have sex in the house, which seemed like a given, but also a total bummer when spoken out loud.

The rest of the house had light switches all over that would turn on flood lights. A list of car makes, models, and license plates were written in pencil in the garage, as though someone had been keeping track of cars coming and going in the neighborhood.

I also found, quite by accident, that the powder room pocket doors were see-through. One did not realize this until one had pulled them shut, dropped trou, and began to turn around and sit down on the toilet. Yes, they were lightly frosted, but no way someone in the living room could not see all your business.

Thinking a warning would have been nice, I asked Mary about this, and she said the doors were that way so the son could see if his mother had fallen in the bathroom.

Our one-hour listing appointment turned into three hours, and I was tired and overwhelmed by Mary's stories. At the end of the tour, I agreed to list the house at a sum that was quite outrageous. But you have to list to last. Mary cautioned me again against having sex in the house (this was really making me want to have sex in the house), leaving any lights on, and making sure all doors were always locked.

Agents who showed the home before had always left lights on, especially upstairs, and she found it very impolite. She had a few lights in the house on timers and that's all she wanted on. Regarding the locks, she said her landscaper had shown up one day and the pedestrian door to the garage was wide open, which, I had to admit, was pretty bad real estate agent form. And a neighbor had seen a man walking out the front door early one morning, and she wasn't sure if he was homeless and had gotten in through an unlocked door or had been having sex with an agent in the house.

As I was leaving, Mary made one more request: Could she have one of those huge, fancy signs with a custom rider that said *indoor pool/sauna*? Of course I said yes. In for a penny, in for an extra hundred bucks. We planned to list the place as soon as the sign came in and have an open house the following Sunday.

I went home and told my husband this whole crazy story. Unlike me, he loves to look at houses and real estate websites in his spare time and was immediately interested in seeing the house. I said only if he promised not to try and have sex with me there. Then I went to the Google to find out if anything Mary told me was true. I tried several search terms, but only managed to pull up a double homicide from the mid-nineties in a different house in the neighborhood. The story itself was awful: An elderly couple went to dinner after being snowed in for several days. Finding the restaurant closed, they returned home and startled two burglars who had been casing their home. In the chaos, one of the burglars shot them both. The couple's daughter had written a lot of blog and message board posts regarding the fact that the shooter was never convicted. She seemed out for vengeance. Maybe this neighborhood just had bad juju.

I didn't know if Mary had heard an altered version of this story or if the car crash really happened. The presence of the indoor pool and wheelchair winch seemed to indicate something did, but I couldn't verify any details. A search of the previous owners' names turned up nothing. However, this crash supposedly happened in the nineties, well before all news was online, so it was possible it was a pre-internet incident.

Figuring there was nothing much to it, I ordered the big, fancy sign and the *indoor pool* rider and waited.

Mary waited, too, but not as patiently. She called daily to see if the sign had arrived, and when it finally did, on a Friday, I told her I was booked all day and couldn't come install it.

"Oh, it's fine if you install it tonight," she said. "As long as it's up by Saturday morning."

After a long day of showing houses, I went home and told my husband I had to drive across town to put a sign out. Since he's a good husband, he rode with me.

We got to the house well after 10 p.m. and started trying to get the sign up. This involved no small amount of cussing, and I was sure someone in this tony enclave would call the police and we would have to go home, but no such luck. We finally got everything put together and in the ground, and my husband really wanted to go see the house. I was tired and hungry and looking for a way to say no when I saw a light on in an upstairs bedroom.

Son of a bitch!

No one had been in to show the house, so Mary must have left it on. But if I didn't turn it off, I would be to blame.

My husband was thrilled at a chance to go in. I went and did my magic with the lockbox, opened the door, and then stood, stock-still next to the man I love. I saw something dart off to the right in the front entryway. Otherwise frozen, my husband and I turned to each other and said, in unison: "Did you see that?" We had both followed it with our heads. I still don't know what "it" was, but immediately knew I didn't like it. In fact, I liked it so little I wanted to drop everything and run away. My husband, however, went after it.

Cursing him and Mary and houses in general, I knew that whatever I had just seen, whatever had made every hair on my body stand on end, I had to turn that goddamn light off upstairs.

Turning on lights, I ran as fast as I could upstairs and searched for the source of the light. I finally found it in a small spare bedroom behind the door that opened to the second floor from the stairwell. It was easy to miss this door with that stairwell door open. I turned it off, leaving the stairwell door open behind me and started back downstairs, only to almost poop my pants when, halfway down, that same stairwell door slammed shut behind me.

My husband was coming around a corner downstairs and I yelled, "Out! Now!" and for once he didn't argue. I locked the door, got in the car, and got the hell out of there.

As we drove away, I rocked back and forth, holding my head, which felt like it was on fire. I didn't know what had just happened, but I knew I never wanted it to happen again. I had just listed this house and never wanted to see it again, much less go inside. And I had an open house on Sunday.

What was I supposed to do? Call Mary and say, "Hey, I'm pretty sure there's some kind of spirit or bad mojo in your house and I can't go back?" Or maybe I could pretend I got hit by a bus.

In the end, the possibility of earning a commission won out. So there I was on Sunday, holding an open house in what I now believed was a haunted house. I had my cupcakes, lemonade, and flyers on standby. I set everything up, including a cute dish towel I had brought to try to brighten up the kitchen, which, in spite of the skylights, seemed dreary and depressing.

I walked in and out of the house a few times to get supplies from my car and every single time I came back in the house that dish towel was on the floor. Not the paper napkins, not the flyers, not the plastic cups or my business cards. Just the dish towel. It was probably nothing, right? Right. My one solace was that I would be out of the house well before it got dark.

Visitors came and everything was going well, except the one time someone tried to use the downstairs bathroom without realizing everyone could see their business. Most people who came were curious neighbors, but that wasn't unusual. Maybe they knew someone who wanted to move near them.

The next-door neighbor was especially chatty.

"My husband and I call this the Amityville Horror House," she told me while taking a bite of her cupcake.

Trying not to seem alarmed, I said, "Oh?" I find that's a good answer for things you don't have good answers for.

"Yeah, because we see lights go on and off all the time, especially upstairs. It's super creepy. Oh! And the owner? That woman? She totally swims naked in that pool at night and you can see everything." The neighbor was smiling and licking frosting off her fingers.

The thought of Mary naked in the pool briefly overshadowed my concern about the lights going on and off upstairs, but not for long. The neighbor, now on a sugar high, left me alone to contemplate everything she had just told me.

Right as the open house was about to end, I got a call from an agent saying she was bringing some clients who were very interested, but they might get there right at 4 p.m. Would I mind waiting? I would, but I told her I would not, because I wanted to sell the damn house.

I wound up alone in the house for a good thirty minutes, as the agent and her clients arrived about 4:15. While it wasn't a creepy wait, it wasn't comfortable.

The agent finally showed up with her clients, who were indeed quite interested, as they had a daughter with physical disabilities and the pool would be perfect for her. This was great news for the sale of the house, but bad news for me trying to get out of there before dark. Meanwhile, the couple wandered around talking about where their furniture would fit and, most importantly, if they could make a bedroom for their daughter on the main floor.

Dusk fell and they were still deliberating. I started making "I have to go" noises, but my desire to make that sweet cash was in direct conflict with my desire to never be in that house alone after dark. Finally, they wrapped it up, just as the sun slipped below the horizon, only a dim glow remaining for me to lock up by.

I literally ran through the house, turning off lights. I had gathered all my open house supplies and put them in the car while the couple had been looking, so that saved some time. Mary had wanted me to turn the lights and jets on in the pool for the open house and turning them off took a while. Standing in the darkening pool area by myself was nerve-wracking. I was in a utility closet, looking for the right buttons and switches to hit and flip while also trying not to think about someone swinging from the kitchen ceiling, lights turning themselves on and off, Mary swimming naked in the pool, and the door that slammed behind me a few short nights ago.

By the time I went to turn the lights off upstairs, it was pitch black. I walked as fast as I could, muttering, "Not today, Satan," under my breath. No doors slammed and I breathed a sigh of relief.

When I was back downstairs, ready to get my keys and turn the final light off in the foyer and lock up, I heard footsteps behind me in the living room. I stopped and the footsteps stopped. Thinking I was imagining things, I kept walking. A few steps later, the footsteps started again. I got that burning feeling on my scalp and all the hairs on my body stood up. I grabbed my keys, pawed at the lights like a wild animal, slammed the front door, locked it, and ran to my car.

The drive home was torture. Was I going crazy? No, my husband had experienced this with me. If I was crazy for anything, it was listing a haunted house and trying to sell a haunted house.

It turned out the buyers who had caused me to stay past dark weren't interested, and Mary, who had fired several listing agents before me, decided I was the reason her house wasn't selling.

She asked me to come to her other house to discuss the situation. I told her I really felt like we needed a price reduction, and she told me I wasn't marketing enough to potential Olympic athletes who would want to use the pool for swim practice. I told her, but only in my head, that she was insane.

This last part was confirmed as I was trying to get out of her personal home. The house she lived in was much less exciting than the haunted pool house but had its quirks. Mary gave me a brief tour, during which I noticed an interesting statue on her mantlepiece. She saw me eyeing it and explained it was Kali, the Hindu goddess of death and destruction. "She also rules over sexuality," she said, a somewhat mad twinkle in her eye.

Wondering who in the hell wants something like that front and center in their living room, I asked to use the bathroom. It was a long drive home and I had had a lot of

Starbucks. As I was washing my hands, I saw small, framed prints on the wall. At first glance they looked like some kind of medieval household scenes. Closer inspection showed tiny devils doing devilish things around the people in the prints. Disconcerted, I just wanted to go home and never see this woman again.

On the way out, because I never know when to get out while the gettin's good, I commented on her sweet kitty, sitting by the front door. Mary told me this cat, Churchill, was still a kitten. I made the appropriate "aw!" noises, and it was then I noticed she was pretty choked up.

"He came to me just after my last cat died," she said, now openly sobbing. "This is the reincarnation of Churchill the First!"

Of course! It made perfect sense that a woman whose dream home featured a sordid backstory, who was totally cool with whatever horrible entity lived in that home, who revered violent goddesses, and who decorated her house with devil-core would believe in reincarnated pets enough to discuss them with her now former real estate agent.

No real estate training had prepared me for this moment, and not knowing what in the world would come out of this woman's mouth next, I made my awkward goodbyes while Mary continued to weep. I fled to my car and sped out of the neighborhood, thanking a non-vengeful god that I would never have to deal with this woman or her haunted house again.

Over the years, I watched that house get relisted with several agents, including the agent she had listed with before who she was sure was fornicating in the house. I never saw it actually sell.

And every time I'm in a house and get a funny feeling or hear or smell something strange, I think of that place. I also drive by sometimes when I'm in the neighborhood showing other houses. I will never know what was truly going on, if there was a restless spirit or if Mary's own energy had funked up the place. What I do know now is that not every commission check is worth it, especially when the signs all point to "Get out!"

And I don't ever want to list another haunted house.

———

SUZY TROTTA *lives in Knoxville, Tennessee, with her husband, their baby angel puppy Jolene, and two cats, Thelma and Louise. She posts personal essays on her site, **www.suzytrotta.com**, and reads them aloud on her podcast, Damn It, Suzy. In addition to writing and podcasting, she spends her time sewing, roller skating, and reading tons of books. She has been a real estate agent for twenty years and is somehow more or less still sane. She looks forward to her eventual literary superstardom and international book tour. A collection of stories about her adventures in real estate will be published by Howling Hills in 2024.*

THE SUSCON SCREAMER

Suscon, Pennsylvania

———

THOM TRACY

Suscon is a remote, wooded place in Northeastern Pennsylvania, where deer, bear, and fresh air are plentiful. This section of Pittston Township exudes peace, but some people might tell you otherwise. Warnings about strange things persist. The legend of the Suscon Screamer has existed for decades. When you talk to people around here, everybody knows something about it—whether or not they believe the various stories. The wailing ghost of a jilted bride. A strange creature shrieking in the night. A tortured soul murdered on prom night.

As a teenager, my reluctance to hang out in Suscon had nothing to do with the Screamer and everything to do with the differences between my pals and the locals. We listened to psychedelic music and wore polo shirts, shorts, and Nikes. The kids up in Suscon loved country music, jeans, boots, and flannel shirts. And there were times, especially at parties, when the factions didn't mix all that well.

Others had their own reasons for avoiding the place.

My dad refused to drive my mom to her best friend's house at the top of Mile Hill, a section of Suscon Road that ascends toward seemingly limitless tracts of forestland. It wasn't a fear of the unknown as much as a fear of sliding off an icy pass or breaking down halfway up the mountain road, miles from help.

Not everyone was as careful. Over the years, people have driven carelessly along the lonely, isolated road that has seen its share of fatal crashes.

Suscon Road crosses over Interstate 81 as it winds southeast toward the Pocono Mountains. About 1.5 miles later, the route takes a sudden, sharp turn to the left. At that point, a railroad overpass loomed for decades until it was torn down in the 1980s. Drivers headed toward that bridge at fast speeds had strong odds of demolishing their cars. To make matters worse, the pavement beneath the bridge narrowed to one lane, and it was difficult to see vehicles coming from the opposite direction.

A version of the Suscon Screamer legend says a bride-to-be was left at the altar before hurrying out of the church. Her last ride counted among the fatal mishaps. Alternate versions are chronicled in two Suscon Screamer books by Stan Zurek. One says she hung herself from the bridge or a tree near the overpass. Another claims the Screamer is the spirit of a mother killed in a crash as she hurried down Mile Hill seeking help for her young daughter, who had drowned in Thornhurst's Mountain Lake. It's since said that stopping under the railroad bridge, flashing your headlights, and honking the horn conjures the specter of a woman in white, screaming malevolently.

Then there's the story of the young girl who found the perfect prom date. He was handsome and charming. After the dance, she agreed to take a ride with him on Suscon Road. Nearby gravel roads make perfect places for teens to be alone. As the story goes, her resistance to his advances was countered by his rage. No one heard her last screams. Somewhere among the pines and rock ledges near the Black Bridge, her body was dumped over an embankment after she'd been sexually assaulted and beaten to death. Travelers near the murder site have claimed to see a woman walking on the berm. Her white-gowned image appears in rearview mirrors and vanishes when occupants try to get a better look. Others remember a female in a white prom dress searching for a ride along Mile Hill. The image appears real at first glance, only to fade from sight as a driver pulls closer.

The Screamer legend has foundations dating to 1946. Where the James A. Musto Bypass exits to the borough of Dupont, you can see hilly terrain that's part of the

Allegheny Plateau. A short hike from Suscon Road as it eases through the 21,137-acre PA State Game Lands 91, Big Shiny Mountain was once the site of a fire tower. Five miles from the Black Bridge, the structure offered a great view of the remote Suscon forest. People who hunt in those woods say anything could be lurking within.

Dupont's late Jim Reap would tell you much the same. Employed in the 1940s as a forest services watcher, he once spotted a mystifying being. In a November 2022 issue of *Greater Pittston Progess*, Dupont historian and retired attorney Jan Lokuta recalls a chat with Reap about the creature's appearance. It was six feet in length with a snout, reddish-brown hair, and eyes that sparkled. The watchman would not see the strange creature again, but he did twice hear unnerving screams, to which a pack of wild dogs would respond in kind. Lokuta thinks it may have been an escaped hyena from an animal exhibit in the Poconos.

That story spawned reports of a similar nature—a howling, tormented bare-skinned creature about the same size as "Reap's monster" approaching a fire tower as another lonely guardsman stood atop the iron lookout. Locking the hatch to the hut atop the tower, he hunkered down and hoped for the best. After a few anxious minutes, he rose and watched the bizarre varmint scramble away from the base of his post. Some figured the thing was a black bear, burned in a brushfire and screaming in pain.

Subsequent sightings of strange beasts could test one's sanity. Unless you've seen Bigfoot. As a nine-year-old,

Wilkes-Barre's Rob Viars saw a bizarre creature walk out of the woods near his home. In a 2019 interview with Philadelphia's WPVI-TV, Viars said three other family members saw the same thing.

"We all ran to the window, and we looked, and the deer had come out of the woods with a creature walking on two legs, really tall and hairy, chasing it across the canal," Viars said.

Eric Altman of the Pennsylvania Cryptozoology Society references reports of Sasquatch sightings that stretch back to the 1800s in lands not far from Suscon. Bigfoot was then known as Wildman.

"The first documented newspaper report of a Wildman sighting came in 1838 up in Bridgewater Township in the northeastern part of the state near the Poconos," Altman said in the same WPVI interview.

Bigfoot clans may have migrated toward Suscon as the years passed. Away from the Pocono region that now serves as a bedroom community for many New York City and New Jersey commuters, the elusive creatures may just desire more solitary space. Many of us can empathize.

Some dismiss the Suscon Screamer. Others feel differently. Believers understand all too well how a lifetime can be spent searching for someone or something to fill a void in the world they know. In a world of which we know nothing, perhaps the search never ends.

THOM TRACY *writes business articles and blog posts for investment sites, insurance businesses, and software companies. He's working on his first nonfiction book,* The Kings of Cork Lane, *a memoir about family and friends written through a baseball lens. He lives in West Pittston, Pennsylvania, and enjoys riding bicycles and collecting pre-war baseball cards.*

— NINETEEN —

A HAUNTING
IN BENT CREEK CEMETERY

Morristown, Tennessee

———

MICHAEL SOBIECH

As a child, I often played with ghosts.

On long summer evenings, my siblings, neighbors, and I played a game of tag, where if you were "it," you faced a tree, covered your eyes, and counted off the hours between 1 p.m. and 11 p.m., ending your chant with one last time marker, followed by a warning: "Midnight! Ghosts in the graveyard!"

As children, we may not have understood a lot, but we knew one thing: Graveyards were for ghosts.

Perhaps as long as people have buried people, there have been stories of the return of the ones buried within, for not all who rest in graves rest in peace—and sometimes the living don't allow the dead to rest in peace.

In December 1953, allegations appeared by mouth and in print that something—or someone—was afoot in a small, country cemetery in Hamblen County, Tennessee. Over the course of weeks, it spiraled into an unsettling experience that turned a community upside down before it was over.

That December, the *Daily Gazette-Mail* of Morristown, Tennessee, reported that something strange was going on in the Whitesburg community, in the vicinity of the historic Bent Creek Cemetery. For weeks, according to the paper, stories circulated about something perhaps not of this world. After weeks of tales, a young Whitesburg resident, Jerry Wilson, and twenty-two employees of Morristown's Berkline furniture company decided to check out the rumors.

On Monday, December 7, about an hour after sunset, Wilson and his friends waited to see what they could see. With a new moon the previous night, the evening would have been dark.

For two hours, nothing happened. But then something did.

At half past 8 p.m., almost two dozen people saw a reddish glow appear. It seemed to come from and hover over one of the graves.

Though scared, the group went toward the phantom light.

The light, though, did not stay put.

As they rushed, it rose—higher and higher.

And then it flew.

The crowd ran to their cars and followed the flying glow a little over three miles to Bulls Gap—and then it disappeared.

The glow was gone, but the news spread quickly: Hamblen County had a haunting.

The next day, people gathered again in growing numbers. One newspaper reported a throng of 500 people and 151 cars gathered at Bent Creek Cemetery to see if the dead had returned to life.

At 8:30 p.m., the crowd's wait was over: Up from a grave a glow arose.

According to observers, it was an object the size of a large grapefruit, a dull red that did not flicker or change. According to Clara Wilson, who lived near the cemetery, the phantom object hovered five stories up, not moving, before eventually, silently, sinking back into the grave from whence it came.

On Wednesday, December 9, it rained. But a thousand people with 200 cars flowed into Bent Creek Cemetery. As on the past nights, they waited. Where was the floating red orb? Lacking an apparition, the crowd turned to conjuring—and gunfire.

According to one newspaper, "some of the ghost hunters called into the cemetery, 'Come on out, damn you, we're ready for you!'" But their words failed. And when words fail in East Tennessee, maybe bullets will succeed: "Shotguns and rifles were in evidence. . . . [and] several fusillades of shots were fired into the cemetery."

Bullets didn't work. The mysterious glow remained below.

But tall tales were spreading, and the crowds grew the next night, with cars from three counties and Kentucky, too. The same for the next night, despite no new sightings.

Those who came were sadly disappointed, as the phenomenon had vanished. What, too, had been the cause? In the long history of ghost stories, ghosts have appeared for a variety of reasons. They appeared because bodies weren't properly buried. They appeared because hearts had been broken. They appeared to right a crime committed against them in life.

The cause of the haunting aside, the gathering crowds wanted answers. On Friday night, December 11, as ghost hunters swarmed to the cemetery, one man changed everything. Instead of a pastor or priest, the man who brought peace was the head of the local police: Hamblen County Sheriff C. L. Franklin.

Sheriff Franklin knew a thing or two about graveyards. Before he became sheriff, he had managed a cemetery. And Franklin knew something about spirits. The pages of the papers often reported on the sheriff and his deputies busting locals for illegal moonshine and alcohol.

Franklin had run for office on the promise to enforce the law. And on Friday night, he personally appeared at Bent

Creek Cemetery. For three hours he "direct[ed] the crowd to keep moving." He told the paper, "I've never seen anything like this ghost business."

When it comes to "ghost business," explanations vary. There are at least three main options.

One, ghosts are real.

Two, the experience is real but there is a normal explanation, rather than paranormal. An example is when Scrooge, in Dickens's *A Christmas Carol*, tells the ghost of Jacob Marley that his dead partner is "...an undigested bit of beef, a blot of mustard, a crumb of cheese, a fragment of underdone potato."

Three, a real experience is traced to a hoax.

In December 1953, people entertained all three options.

For some, the glow was a ghost.

For others, the glow was a gas—nothing more than a will-o'-the-wisp. According to this unproven theory, decomposition produces methane gas, which somehow ignites.

The Christmas Eve edition of the *Rogersville Review* offered another natural explanation: The mysterious light might be an airplane beacon. The paper interviewed S. C. Roberts, who lived near Bent Creek. Roberts didn't think the glow was anything supernatural; he pointed out that an airplane beacon was located a mile away from the graveyard. Perhaps the red glow had something to do with that.

But for others, the glow was a prank. Perhaps it was a boy with a flashlight. Perhaps it was a prankster's balloon covered with luminous paint.

In the end, the hoax explanation spelled the end for the Bent Creek Cemetery ghost. Sheriff Franklin believed neighborhood boys were behind it, telling *The Morristown Sun*, "It is just a hoax."

The police don't stop all pranks, nor do they put an end to everything that might or might not be a hoax. So why this one?

Because the sheriff stood in the cemetery that Friday night. Over the course of five nights, hundreds and hundreds of people and hundreds of cars had poured into the rain-drenched paths of a small graveyard. Over the course of five nights, people had set off fireworks, lit gunpowder on tombstones, and people shot guns into the cemetery itself.

For three hours Sheriff Franklin stood and watched a sacred place become a circus. He brought the "haunting" to an end with these poignant words: "The people at Whitesburg are fed up with all the curiosity seekers desecrating the cemetery."

The Bent Creek Cemetery haunting is an episode that reminds us the dead are not always the most frightful threat. With throngs of people trampling on sacred ground, shooting off fireworks, firing guns, a lawman recognized the real threat in Bent Creek Cemetery: the living to the dead.

A version of this essay was first presented at the 2022 Mildred Haun Conference (Walters State Community College). Quotations and details are taken or adapted from contemporary reports in several area newspapers: Daily Gazette-Mail (*Morristown*), Sunday Gazette-Mail (*Morristown*), Rogersville Review, The Morristown Sun, The Greeneville Sun, The Knoxville News-Sentinel. *All newspapers were accessed via Newspapers.com. For a full list of citations, please contact the author at msobiech@cn.edu.*

———

MICHAEL SOBIECH *is an associate professor of English at Carson-Newman University, where he directs the first-year writing program and the professional writing minor. Dr. Sobiech researches Appalachian folklore with a focus on ghost stories. "Ghosts in a Graveyard: A Haunting in Bent Creek Cemetery" stems from his 2021 sabbatical project, which involved examining historical East Tennessee newspapers for allegedly true tales of the paranormal. Mike likes to hike, read, write, and take photos of the great outdoors. His only claim to fame is that he once shook hands with Vincent Price.*

No.

— TWENTY —

MR. OLDFIELD'S GIFT

Rugby, Tennessee

———

JEANNETTE BROWN

I have only myself to blame. I dithered around too long before registering for a writing workshop in a nearby ghost town, led by a Famous Writer. I was thinking "yes" to opportunities for adventure and "no" to being judged by writers who were possibily better than me. Also, I believe in, and therefore fear, ghosts. That factored in my procrastination, but what got my check in the mail was my fear of never becoming a Famous Writer.

The payback is I am the last to register and thus will take the last room and thus will be sharing a bath. Yes, the other

rooms come with baths, but not mine and not the one
reserved by the next-to-the-last reservee. A man. A stranger.

The last man I shared a bath with was my ex-husband.
It did not go well. One minute I finished cleaning the
bathroom, the next, he's turned it into a toxic waste center.
(That's not the reason he's my ex, but we can agree it was
a contributing factor.) My best writing/thinking happens
while in the small room. The last thing I need is a strange
man banging on the door because I'm spending too long in
there.

Still, I drive two hours to a ghost town to stay in a ghost
house with a bunch of ghost writers. Ha! That's not true,
although it might be once I meet everyone. There'll be
six students and one Famous Writer and her assistant.
Probably mostly females except my bath-mate. I almost
back out, but there's this one piece of writing, a short story
with great potential, that I can't seem to find the core
of and I'm hoping this workshop will solve the problem.
Or convince me to trash it and begin something worth
finishing. I will trust the judgment of the Famous Writer.

Located down a lonely country road, the retreat
destination—Newbury House in Rugby, Tennessee—looks
benign enough. I am calmed by the wrap-around porch, its
curtains flapping from second-story windows. If there are
ghosts, I'm sure they are benevolent ones.

The house, built in 1880, smells like it. I can almost see
the ancestral DNA floating about. The assistant shows me
to my room at the top of the stairs, apologizing for the

shared bathroom. Each bedroom is named for a settler of the town, now ghosts themselves. I'll sleep beneath Emily Hughes, whose photograph hangs above the bed. I have my very own, personal ghost. She looks wholesome. The typed bio on the dresser says she died in a foreign country. I hope that means she's haunting some place in Chile or Chad and not here. If I weren't so superstitious, I'd read up on the factors that determine where and when and why a ghost haunts.

The assistant gives a brief description of the other rooms, but the one that snags my attention is Room Number 2, the Charles Oldfield Room. This is the lodging of my male bath sharer. It is also the room with the most interesting ghost, as Mr. Oldfield actually died in that room, if not that bed. On the desk, a sepia photo of Charles Oldfield shows an older, unsmiling man from the 1880s, with a receding hairline and muttonchop sideburns. I make a fierce face back at him. His typed bio explains he was miffed because, when he was deathly ill, his wife refused to leave England to be by his side and care for him. Behind cupped hand, the assistant reports that Mr. Oldfield continues to frequent the room. He probably also frequents the shared bathroom. I shiver at the thought.

I gather with the others in the downstairs parlor. Lit by table lamps, the corners of the room remain in shadow. The air is stuffy and heavy like that of an antique store, which this parlor really is, filled with rigid, red-brocade, horsehair settees. Settees is my grandmother's word for sofas. She, too, is an antique.

A distinctive energy fills the room. It speaks of hope and creativity and uncertainty. I see two women—another one is late due to car trouble—and two men. They are both of a certain age (mine) and look well-mannered enough. I hope their moms or wives taught them bathroom etiquette.

In the "getting to know you" circle, I report that I've had a few stories published and have an idea for a novel, but the reason I'm here—Famous Writer cuts me off to finish getting to know the others. I hope this doesn't portend the future of this weekend, especially considering that I've submitted what I have of my story for Famous Writer's critique.

Dinner is convivial enough, served with wine and literary gossip; authors swapping partners or losing publishing contracts because they plagiarized. Upstairs, a door slams. I flinch, alert for the sound of footsteps. No one else seems to have heard it. No one is missing. I chat with one of the men. He smells good. I hope he is my bath-mate, but no, he's in Room 3, that of Sarah Hughes, Emily's great aunt. Comes with private bath. The other man, (I'll call him Bill) seems nice enough. A little taken aback when I joke about sharing the bathroom.

The evening ends with the passing of the wine bottle on the front porch of Newbury House, listening to the creak of the porch-swing chain and rocking chairs. It's twilight. Here in the countryside, I can see stars and meteors and other astrological events. No one talks.

The stairs to the second floor are narrow, so I hold onto the wall, placing my feet carefully. I flinch as my hand touches a cold spot on the wallpaper. I pat the spaces around the spot. They are all warm. Then the cold patch again. I ignore it and keep going up.

In bed, my unfinished story surfaces, haunting me again. I'm trying to write a light little romance, but it keeps going dark on me. Car wrecks. Downed electrical lines. Keys dropped overboard into a lake. Finally, sleep comes, but I burst awake at the sound of moaning. I go to the door to listen, but there's nothing. It must have been something I dreamt. Or ate. Or drank.

I sleep dreamlessly until my alarm makes that nuclear sub noise. I dress hurriedly and hope the bathroom is empty. It is, but with the aroma of someone who's inhabited it recently.

The afternoon is free for our writing. My short story sits on the page like a clump of raw dough. It needs baking. I close my eyes to attract the muse, but Mr. Charles Oldfield wafts through my brain. My story is not getting written because his—a dark romance—takes up so much room. I've heard it's better not to push the writing, just wait for it to form. Putting down my pen, I peer out the window at the splendid autumn day. Perhaps a walk will bring inspiration.

In the hall I am waylaid by Famous Author, who has comments on my story. I take a deep breath and accept whatever she has to offer instead of putting up my usual invisible shield in the face of criticism. But I can't help thinking that, considering the price of the weekend package, I deserve at least fifteen minutes with her in a private room.

"It's fine. It's a good story. A little dark."

Famous Author or Famous Witch? How would she know the ending to my unfinished short story?

I swing by the kitchen to grab a paper cup and an open bottle of wine. The assistant mentions a winery down the road. I don't ask whether it, too, is haunted.

It's autumn, a seasonal mix of dead leaves and spider webs. The scum on the Adirondack chair doesn't dissuade me from sitting. A slight breeze shimmers through the water. An extraordinarily large frog belches out a tune. Maybe I'll sit here through the evening session, all the way past dinner. The time changed last week, but my body hasn't adjusted. Only the darkness will convince me.

Autumn is necessarily melancholy. I try not to sink into it, remembering all my mistakes, my bad choices, my regrets. Maybe I should switch stories, choose someone else's darkness. Choose one of those poor souls underground in the nearby cemetery and fashion a story of their failure, either from typhus or lack of farming expertise.

A luminous full moon hangs just outside my bedroom window. I can almost see the last of the Halloween witches floating by on their brooms traveling to make mischief. I'll never get to sleep with that light shining on my face. I pull the curtains.

As I drift into slumber, the perfect ending to my story appears as if it were hovering over my head. I consider rising to find paper and pen, so it doesn't escape, but it's so perfect I'll surely remember it in the morning. I exhale. Relax. Nothing to worry about now. I settle into a deep sleep. REMs. Sawing logs. Goldilocks.

As dawn breaks, I'm awakened by the sound of voices in the hall. Opening the door, I see most of our group huddled around Bill's/Charles Oldfield's room. People are murmuring "odd" and "strange." Making my way into the room, I see the bedcovers are hastily thrown back, as if someone had a sudden urge to visit the bathroom. Or, as the assistant describes it, "like he'd seen a ghost."

I notice the picture of Mr. Oldfield face down on the desk. I sympathize with Bill. Who could sleep with that staring at you?

But then I see something that sends chills up my spine: two wine glasses on the dresser are precariously tilted toward each other, as if glued at the rims. I hold my breath as if my exhale would cause them to pull apart and shatter.

Famous Author has found a note from Bill. An emergency at home requires his presence, but no need for us to worry. I don't believe him, not with the energy I feel in this room, vibrant yet foreboding.

I make my way through the cluster of writers and down the hall. The bathroom is empty. It's all mine now.

JEANNETTE BROWN*'s work has been in* Bellevue Literary Review, Southwestern American Literature, Descant, Steel Toe Review, *and other publications. She is co-editor of* Literary Lunch, *a food anthology. She has enjoyed residencies at the Sewanee Writers' Conference, Rivendell Writers' Colony, and Hedgebrook/India. Her novel,* The Illusion of Leaving, *was published by Texas Review Press. Her play,* Cuba Libre, *is in development with the Tennessee Stage Company.*

— TWENTY-ONE —

THE ATTIC

Fountain City, Tennessee

———

CANDANCE REAVES

It was the perfect house, a 1925 bungalow with almost an acre of land and a small barn. The property had once been a larger working farm with cattle and a big garden, but suburban sprawl had whittled it down to its current size. All the house needed was some cosmetic upgrades and better landscaping. We were anxious to get started.

On move-in day, the former owner came and handed us the extra set of keys. As she was leaving, she said, "Oh, by the way, the house comes with a ghost. My daughter used to hear footsteps coming down the hallway to her bedroom."

Then she was gone.

We were too busy over the next few weeks to think about what she had said. My husband, John, forgot entirely. He was reminded late one night while grading essays in his office, the daughter's room. I was reminded when he came up to our bedroom, woke me and asked if I had come down the hallway a few minutes earlier. I said, no, that I was asleep. He told me he had been in his office when he heard me walking down the hall and stopping in the doorway. He turned to see what I wanted, but no one was there. My groggy face told him all he needed to know. It wasn't me.

My husband chalked it up to his own exhaustion from having graded papers most of the night. Being me, I thought he heard the footsteps the daughter had often heard. I had seen enough ghost hunting shows to know this particular occurrence was probably a residual haunt— sounds so ingrained in the walls that they repeat themselves over and over through the years. I told John this and got the usual look that told me it was nonsense. Okay, noted.

It wasn't long before I had my own unexplained occurrence. I was in the downstairs bathroom opposite the attic stairs. I was washing my hands and heard distinct footsteps coming down the stairs. They were carpeted, so the sound had to be pretty distinct to be heard. I opened the door expecting to see John, but no one was there. I called out to him, and he answered from the breakfast room in the kitchen. I went into the kitchen and asked if he had just come down the stairs from our room. No, he had not. I went to find our cats, and they were in their usual spots on the couch in the living room, sound asleep. I walked back into the kitchen, looked at John, shook my head and walked back into the hallway and up the stairs to my office. No one there, of course. I started to rethink our purchase of the house. I am not one of those people who thinks it's cool to live in a haunted house. I can watch it on TV and know in my heart it is somehow staged. But to have it happen to me with no explanation? Nah.

One day John was mowing the lawn when he saw the elderly neighbor across the road out in his yard. John stopped the mower to go and introduce himself. Mr. Willson was a fixture around Fountain City in years past. My father had bought meat for his restaurant from him for years. Mr. Willson asked John if he enjoyed the house. Yes, he said, and told him about the garden. Mr. Willson said the original owners were the Claboughs and that the husband fixed autos. That explained all the mufflers in the loft. Somehow, we never needed a muffler for a '45 Ford truck. Mr. Willson also told John "the old man," as he called him, was "the strangest son of a bitch" he ever knew and that the Claboughs were ultrareligious and locked their sons in the attic for even small infractions. The old man didn't trust banks and had hidden money on the property. The former owner did tell us they found a floor safe in one side of the attic upstairs behind the knee wall.

Small things continued to happen in the night. John told me he didn't like sitting in the breakfast room then because he always got the feeling someone was watching him from inside the house. I was sitting in the living room one night and saw out of the corner of my eye what I thought were a man's black shoes in the doorway from the dining room. When I turned and looked full on, they were gone.

Things ramped up one night just before Halloween. I went upstairs and into the attic to retrieve decorations for the front door, pulling the small door shut behind me so the cats would not follow. I rummaged around for the box, found it and attempted to back out of the door. It wouldn't budge. I set the box down and tried again to get the door open. Again, it would not budge. I hadn't locked it. You couldn't lock it from inside the attic. You had to maneuver a sliding latch on the outside of the door into a hole in the frame.

I yelled for John.

"Where are you?" came the reply from downstairs.

"I'm in the attic," I shouted.

"Where?" John yelled as he came up the stairs.

"In the attic."

"How did you lock yourself in the attic?" he asked when he reached the door.

"I didn't. Mr. Clabough did," I said, trying to keep things light. I heard him slide the bolt from the frame and the door opened. He had a puzzled look on his face. Mine must have been white.

"How did you do that?"

"I told you, I didn't. I just pulled it closed to keep the cats out." He must have tried to get the door to lock by itself for a good ten minutes. He shook it, slid the lock over just to the hole, shook it again, didn't shake it but just closed it, and made several other attempts to get it to lock. You could not get the bolt to slide into the wall without physically moving it there. Even then, you had to lift it up out of its notch and slide it.

This happened to me twice more. At Christmas when I was getting those decorations out, I had to yell for my mother's friend, Jean, who was downstairs with her wrapping gifts. Jean did not suffer fools and was not going to let that lock stump her. She tried for at least twenty minutes with the same results as John. She just looked at me and shook her head.

"Don't tell Mom," I said.

And it happened one last time. I checked the lock before I went in. It was in its notch all the way to the left. I even put a piece of cardboard between the door and the jamb to keep it shut but not locked. When I tried the door, it was the same as before—locked tight. When John got me out, the cardboard was on the outside on the floor.

"Don't ever go in there when I'm not at home."

"Not a chance," was all I said.

The weird sounds and happenings finally stopped after I read in the obituaries that Mr. Clabough's wife had passed away at the age of 99. Mr. Clabough must have finally crossed over to be with her.

———

CANDANCE REAVES *has been published in* New Millennium Writings, Still: The Journal, Motif: Writing by Ear, Homeworks: A Book of Tennessee Writers, Appalachian Life Magazine *and several anthologies by The Knoxville Writers Guild. She lives near the Great Smoky Mountains where she finds a lot of her inspiration for writing.*

— TWENTY-TWO —

SINGER IN THE WOODS

Wyoming County, West Virginia

———

SHERRY POFF

My dad was a down-to-earth, tell-the-truth kind of man. He was the oldest of eight brothers, and they all grew up hoeing a row almost as soon as they could hold the tools. He spent four grueling years in the Army during World War II and returned home to the coal mines. By the time I was old enough to hear the story I am retelling here, Daddy had been a Baptist deacon and a Sunday School teacher for more than a decade. Though he was a jokester and loved to spin a tale, Daddy always got serious when recounting this story.

Daddy and his brothers were fox hunters—the kind who camp out all night on a mountain top, sitting around a fire listening to the dogs run the fox and calculating whose hound is leading by each one's distinguishing bark. Their dad, my Grandpa Sherman, passed along his love of the chase to his sons, and they found frequent opportunities to take a break from work on the farm to enjoy this recreation in their native hills of southern West Virginia.

One evening in late spring, Daddy and a couple of his brothers were leading the hounds along a dirt road through the woods, headed for a favorite campsite, when they heard singing. Stopping the dogs to listen, the brothers recognized the song: "Amazing Grace." The clear notes of a woman's voice were accompanied by the clip-clop of a horse's hooves and seemed to be not far behind them on the road.

After a short conversation, the young men decided to lead their dogs into the woods so as not to spook the horse. They descended the bank below the road and waited among the trees and leaf litter for the rider to pass. With a clear view of the road, the trio waited and watched expectantly as the sounds of singing and hoof beats drew ever closer.

When the singer was seemingly right above them on the road, the dogs began straining at their leashes and whimpering, eyes fixed on the roadway. The men, however, did not see what their ears were telling them should have been there. Neither the horse nor the rider was visible to the men. They still heard the strains of the old hymn; they clearly discerned the horse's footfall on the roadway, but they did not see any living being pass by. As the sounds faded away, men and dogs scurried back up the bank and into the road where they saw no sign of anyone's passing.

Years later, my dad still told this story in hushed tones and with tears brimming his eyes. He never tried to offer an explanation for this strange encounter, but his belief in the event was steadfast. "We had trouble holding the dogs," he explained. "They seemed to see something we couldn't see, or maybe they were just as confused as we were. One thing is sure, we didn't imagine it. Something was there."

––––––

SHERRY POFF *grew up in the hills of West Virginia. She now lives and writes in and around Chattanooga, Tennessee, where she interacts with a large group of students and family members. She holds an MA in Writing from the University of Tennessee at Chattanooga and is a member of the Chattanooga Writers' Guild. Her stories and poems have appeared recently in the* Anthology of Appalachian Writers, Stone Poetry Journal, *and* Pine Mountain Sand and Gravel. *Her short poem "Resurrection" was nominated for the Pushcart Prize.*

— TWENTY-THREE —

THE RAVEN MOCKER

Knoxville, Tennessee

———

KIMBERLY L. BECKER

I was working as a hospice chaplain, based in Knoxville, Tennessee, and traveling twelve counties. My patients were sometimes in facilities and sometimes at home. I got an admission for an elderly lady, whose historic house, more of a cottage, was tucked into the side of a hill, surrounded by trees. As I pulled up, I admired the long, covered porch with its cozy rockers. I lowered my car window for some air as I turned on my tablet and opened her chart to start my visit, which would need to be at least forty-five minutes to be billable. With the window down, I could hear the faint sound of water (there must have been a hidden stream nearby, and we weren't far from the river) and the call of what sounded like a raven. Such smart birds. I would often see and hear them in my mother's yard. I'd seen videos of how they could even mimic human speech. I gathered my tablet and keys, as well as my cell phone.

As a hospice chaplain I supported the emotional and spiritual lives of terminally ill patients. I often assisted in "life review" and in meaning-making: that is, helping patients go back over their lives and find meaning as they prepared for death. I was also there to support family members as they prepared emotionally for the death of their loved one.

I worked as part of a team that also had nurses, certified nursing assistants, and social workers, all headed up by a physician. Our goal was to provide palliative care to attend to the emotional, spiritual, and physical needs of our patients as they transitioned into the active dying phase. We met once a week to discuss each patient. It was sacred work and I loved it. The pay was low, but the reward was great. Far from finding it depressing, I derived much satisfaction from helping people find a measure of peace at the end of their lives, and I had been privy to more than one deathbed confession.

Like others on my team, I considered death to be like birth on the other side of the spectrum. Some people have what we called good deaths, peaceful release. Others, while comfortable physically thanks to medication, still struggled emotionally or spiritually to let go. As the team chaplain, I would often get a referral to these patients.

My patient's room was at the back of the house. Her daughter led me through a living room filled with Native American art and objects, back to the bedroom, which was dimly lit, and where I saw a frail old woman in bed, covered in quilts, her long white hair in a braid that snaked over her pillow. A tray of uneaten food was beside her.

Her daughter went around to sit in the chair beside the bed and tried to coax a bite of what appeared to be pudding into her mother's mouth. The patient did not open her mouth; instead, she was staring at me. She looked scared and the room felt very cold. No wonder she needed all those quilts, even though it was a hot summer day outside. It is common for those near death to refuse food. The body is shutting down and doesn't need the sustenance. This can be distressing to families who want to feed their loved ones or have them take "just a sip" of water.

The daughter did not force the food. Instead, she kissed her mother on the top of her head and said, "This lady chaplain is here to visit with you, Mama." To me, she said as she went by, "She hasn't been talking, just staring like she sees something that's not there. She keeps pointing to the corner of her room, but I keep telling her there's nothing there. Let me know if you need anything. I have work calls to make."

She left, shutting the door behind her.

I shivered, despite the heat outdoors. I glanced down at my tablet to remind myself of the woman's name and age, in her nineties. There was nothing in her chart about any religion, but I saw she was Cherokee, a part of my heritage. So something made me say hello in Cherokee: "Siyo."

Her face, previously impassive, lit up. She whispered a "siyo" in return.

I knew very little of the language, but I told her my name, "Kim dagwadoa."

She gave a barely perceptible nod. She pulled the quilts up tighter around her.

"It *is* cold in here, isn't it?" Then I told her I was there to listen to anything she might want to talk about or just to sit with her.

She answered, "Pray."

I didn't know if that was a question or a statement, so I said, yes, we could pray. As soon as we mentioned prayer, the room darkened. I realized then it was a just a lightbulb on her nightstand that was flickering out. I went over and, using a tissue so as not to get burned, tightened the bulb in its socket, but the bulb had burnt out. The shades were drawn so now the only light came from around the edges of the windowsill.

Suddenly her hand, thin and mottled with age, reached from under her quilt to grab my wrist. "Pray," she said, and there was fear in her voice. She held my wrist with surprising strength until I lowered myself into the chair her daughter had vacated.

"Of course, we can pray. What would you like to pray for?" I never presumed to pray without asking that question; who was I to impose prayers on the dying?

She pointed to her heart, anxiously looking toward the corner of her room, eyes wide in what seemed to be rising terror. I felt prickles on my skin. I had read in her chart that one of her co-morbidities was congestive heart failure. Praying for her heart made sense. She then said, "tsalagi."

Was she wanting me to pray in Cherokee? I told her my language wasn't very good, but that I would pray what prayers I knew in our language, thankful for my immersion class a few years before.

"Sgi Unetlvna," I began (Thank you, Creator).

A floorboard creaked as though someone were in the room.

As I began to pray, tears started to flow down her face. I didn't know her history. For all I knew she had been sent to government boarding schools, where Native language was forbidden. The ghost of racism still haunted this country that was founded on genocide, built on slavery. She was gripping my hand now and trembling so hard that at first I thought she might be having a seizure. I scanned her chart for any mention of epilepsy, but there was none. As I continued to pray with what Cherokee I knew, adding English when I got stuck, I felt pressure against me, increasing to the point that I momentarily wondered if I were the one having some kind of medical incident, but my patient pointed a thin shaking finger toward the same corner.

When I turned to look, I saw a massive black shadow extending from ceiling to floor, emanating from the corner of the room, so that as the shadow spread it looked like giant wings about to enfold both me and my patient. That was when I knew what this was, what we were dealing with, a name that should never even be spoken. I knew there was a malevolent Cherokee force that hovered in the rooms of the dying, waiting to take the heart from the body to extend its own life.

I remembered reading what ethnologist James Mooney had written about them:

"Of all the Cherokee witches the most dreaded is the Raven Mocker... the one that robs the dying of life... when someone is sick or dying... the Raven Mocker goes to the place to take the life. He flies through the air... with arms outstretched like wings... makes a cry like the cry of a raven as it 'dives' in the air... and those who hear are afraid... When the Raven Mocker comes to the house he finds others of his kind waiting there and unless there is a doctor on guard who knows how to drive them away they go inside, all invisible, and frighten and torment the sick man until they kill him... After the witches kill him they take out his heart and eat it, and so add to their own lives... there is no scar where they take out the heart... Only one who has the right medicine can recognize a Raven Mocker, and if such a man stays in the room with the sick person these witches... retreat as soon as they see him, because when one of them is recognized in his right shape he must die within seven days."

I kept praying, knowing I was mispronouncing some Cherokee words my teacher had taught me, but knowing my intentions to comfort my patient were good. Gradually the pressure receded, and the shadow retracted as I raised my voice (whether verbally or just in my mind, I can't recall) to the shadow figure, *I know who you are and you cannot be here; you cannot have her heart. Leave her to die in peace!*

I was in cold sweat and had not yet begun to chart anything about this bizarre visit. I had no idea what time it was and couldn't check, as my patient still held my hand even as she had somehow managed to fall asleep. The presence had not left completely, but it was no longer rearing above us in vast shadow and I could sense its power weakening after being named and recognized and told to leave.

I remembered how once, when I had been dying of a then-undiagnosed illness, a figure of light had sat by my bedside and brushed my arm with its limb of light. I was feverish so yes, it could have been a hallucination, but I had always interpreted it as reassurance from another source that I would survive. In this room, though, death was imminent, and the presence was not one of light, but of darkness. My patient had fallen into a deep sleep. I prayed and held the presence at bay until suddenly it was gone, no longer smothering the room with its evil force.

Then, a tap at the bedroom door before the daughter entered again, whispering surprise that her mother was finally resting: "She hasn't slept like that in days, even with the medication."

I slipped my hand from my patient's hand gently, so as not to wake her, then quietly exited the room with the daughter, pushing the door closed behind me after nervously checking the corner for any remaining shadow. I could feel my shirt sticking to my back. I felt exhausted. As I turned to walk back down the hall, I felt it again at my back pushing me, hard.

I turned to face a large black mass that had no form or rather no firm form. It was again a large dark presence overshadowing me. The daughter seemed not to see or notice anything amiss, but she did ask if I had forgotten something, since I had stopped in my tracks. I felt weakened from previous prayers and efforts and wished that I could stay and keep watch, but I had other patients to get to. The daughter had already gone ahead to the living room.

I hissed at the form, *I told you I know what you are, and you are not welcome here! Get out in the name of Creator and all that is good. Leave this woman and this place that has been blessed with prayer.*

I don't know if I said these words aloud or just thought them, but the form shrank back and I suddenly felt very faint, as though I had just physically exerted myself, although I knew then it had been a spiritual battle between forces of good and evil.

The daughter called from the living room, "Can I get you some water before you leave? I know it's hot out."

I said yes, thank you, and accepted the cool water gratefully.

The daughter then asked if I had any recommendations to help her mother.

Looking at all the Native art and objects, I said to pray and burn some cedar and tobacco in her mother's room if she had it.

She said her mother had always followed traditional ways and was "superstitious."

I said it was important to validate her mother's beliefs. Since the daughter seemed skeptical, I decided not to share what I had experienced. I decided she wouldn't believe it anyway. I could barely believe it myself. I felt completely drained.

The daughter showed me out. I crossed the porch and descended the steps. When I got to my car, I turned to look back and saw a cat sitting at the door. I laughed to myself. Of course, the cat was black. It was washing its face then stopped to regard me with gold, impassive eyes. For a moment, I remembered shapeshifting, but dismissed it. I sat in my car for a few minutes, wondering how I could possibly chart visit notes. "Patient is beginning to transition. CH provided spiritual care and anxiety-relief in form of prayer in PT's Native language and awareness of cultural tradition."

My patient died within a couple days. I drove past her house a month or so later. When I had made a bereavement call to the daughter, she said she was prepping the house for selling. She had only been there caring for her mother, but was now returning to her home out West, in Arizona, I think.

To write all this down doesn't seem real. I am sure many will doubt what I have tried to describe. I may not be the most reliable narrator, since I was so focused on fighting that negative force that I might be exaggerating my own role. I didn't feel like I did anything other than respond to what was before me and try to validate my patient's spiritual experience. I was grateful to have even the slimmest cultural ties that enabled me to provide some comfort to her at the end of her earthly life. I am not a medicine person. I have no special powers except for faith. I am not an enrolled member of a sovereign nation. But I remembered some prayers in Cherokee to soothe my patient and thankfully had recognized the threat to her, as vulnerable as she was, being so close to death. I was humbled to have been able to serve, but I pray I never encounter such a malevolent power again.

————

The Great Smoky Mountains are a mountain range rising along the Tennessee–North Carolina border in the southeastern United States. They are a subrange of the Appalachian Mountains, and form part of the Blue Ridge Physiographic Province.

Dedicated to the memory of Sequoyah Guess (United Keetoowah Band of Cherokee Indians), founding member of The Turtle Island Liars Club, whose own book Kholvn explores the Cherokee legend of the Raven Mocker, an evil entity who preys on the sick and dying. I am grateful for the advice he gave me on choosing a path to follow: red or white. I chose and choose red.

With gratitude, as always, to Shawn Crowe (Eastern Band of Cherokee Indians), first reader and cultural advisor on this story. Thank

you for having invited me to write for you—and for Cherokee Youth in
Radio.

Thank you also to my language teacher, Bo Taylor (EBCI), who
taught me how to pray in Cherokee and whose admonition I have never
forgotten: "You can't be part Cherokee; you either are or you aren't. But
if you say you are, I'm going to expect something of you." I hope my
writing in some way honors the Cherokee in me.

———

Reference: Cherokee History, Myths, and Sacred Formulas by James
Mooney

———

Of mixed descent, including Cherokee, **KIMBERLY L.**
BECKER *is author of five poetry collections:* Words Facing East *and*
The Dividings *(WordTech Editions),* The Bed Book *and* Bringing Back
the Fire *(Spuyten Duyvil), and* Flight *(MadHat Press). Her work appears*
widely, including in Indigenous Message on Water; Women Write
Resistance: Poets Resist Gender Violence; Tending the Fire: Native
Voices and Portraits, *and* Unpapered: Writers Consider Native
American Identity and Cultural Belonging *(University of Nebraska*
Press). She has served as mentor for PEN America's Prison Writing and
AWP's Writer to Writer programs. A transplant from North Carolina,
she now lives in North Dakota.

We hope you were thrilled, intrigued, and moved by

2*3*tales

**APPALACHIAN GHOST STORIES,
LEGENDS & OTHER MYSTERIES**

Howling Hills is proud to preserve these odd and haunting stories through the work of some fine writers.

We enjoyed it so much we want to do it again. Next year, we plan to publish *24 Tales: More Appalachian Ghost Stories, Legends, and Mysteries.*

We'll begin accepting submissions for the 2024 anthology soon. Visit *www.howlinghillspublishing.com* and follow us on social for more details. We welcome your feedback, so feel free to reach out at *terry@howlinghillspublishing.com* and *brad@howlinghillspublishing.com*.

Thanks for reading, and thanks for supporting independent book publishing.

TERRY SHAW *and* BRAD LIFFORD
Howling Hills Publishing

24 tales

MORE APPALACHIAN GHOST STORIES, LEGENDS & OTHER MYSTERIES

EDITED BY
TERRY SHAW & BRAD LIFFORD

HOWLING HILLS PUBLISHING

East Tennessee

GARDEN STORIES

Sharing Knowledge, Celebrating Heritage, and Building Community

THROUGH THIS BOOK, WE WANT TO GROW THE LOVE OF GARDENING STORY BY STORY.

Visit a gardener, and you'll take away something of value. It might be a different way of seeing things or maybe something to avoid. To write this book, we visited a lot of them. Here are just a few:

- A minister who feed souls and an inner-city community through BattleField Farms

- A poet whose garden inspires her creativity

- Teens who preserve an antebellum garden at Kingsport's Exchange Place, including an obscure plant that tastes like oysters

- A woodland gardener who grows several species of trillium behind her house

Sharing garden stories is the essence of *East Tennessee Garden Stories*. More than that, we're sharing people stories—the kind we hope can help build community, neighborhood by neighborhood, county by county, and region by region.

www.ingramcontent.com/pod-product-compliance
Lightning Source LLC
Chambersburg PA
CBHW070113030426

42335CB00016B/2133